THE DRONER'S MANUAL

Kevin **JENKINS**

THE DRONER'S
MANUAL

A Guide to the Responsible Operation
of Small Unmanned Aircraft

AVIATION SUPPLIES & ACADEMICS, INC | NEWCASTLE, WASHINGTON

The Droner's Manual: A Guide to the Responsible Operation of Small Unmanned Aircraft
by Kevin Jenkins

Aviation Supplies & Academics, Inc.
7005 132nd Place SE
Newcastle, Washington 98059-3153
asa@asa2fly.com | www.asa2fly.com

Cover photos: Images used under license from Shutterstock.com. *Front cover (top) and back cover:* Alexey Yuzhakov/Shutterstock.com. *Front cover (bottom):* Volodymyr Goinyk/Shutterstock.com.

ASA-UAS-DRONE
ISBN 978-1-61954-433-8

Printed in the United States of America.
2021   2020   2019   2018   9   8   7   6   5   4   3   2

Library of Congress Cataloging-in-Publication Data
Names: Jenkins, Kevin (Aerospace engineer), author.
Title: The droner's manual: a guide to the responsible operation of small unmanned
    aircraft / Kevin Jenkins.
Identifiers: LCCN 2017027598 | ISBN 9781619544338 (trade pbk.: alk. paper) |
    ISBN 1619544334 (trade pbk.)
Subjects: LCSH: Drone aircraft—Handbooks, manuals, etc. | Vehicles, Remotely
    piloted—Handbooks, manuals, etc.
Classification: LCC TL685.35 .J46 2017 | DDC 629.132/529—dc23
LC record available at https://lccn.loc.gov/2017027598

Contents

About the Author

Kevin Jenkins grew up outside of Portland, Oregon, near the airport where he first learned to fly. In 2009, he earned a degree in Aerospace Engineering from Embry-Riddle Aeronautical University in Prescott, Arizona. Kevin spent several years as a test engineer and UAV operator, including deployments to Iraq and Afghanistan. After returning to the United States, he worked on a composites research and development team but was soon drawn back into the field of unmanned aircraft. What began as

a hobby in his garage developed into a full-time career, leading to positions with three small companies developing small UAVs for civilian applications. Kevin is deeply passionate about the science of unmanned flight and its potential to shape the world we live in.

Introduction

RC Aircraft, Drones, and UAVs

With the rise of civilian unmanned aviation, several terms have entered the public vocabulary which are, in many cases, falsely considered synonymous. Therefore, it is important to establish, at least within the framework of this book, what each of the terms mean, beginning with the one that is probably most familiar to the layperson.

A remote control or radio control (RC) aircraft is an aircraft, regardless of size, that is piloted solely by a person outside of that aircraft via some means of wireless communication. While some advanced RC systems are capable of transmitting basic information (such as battery voltage or signal strength) back to the pilot, communication is more commonly entirely one-way, with the pilot sending commands to the aircraft. These aircraft are not capable of autonomous flight, and the act of flying an RC aircraft is a finely honed skill. It is important to understand RC flight as many conventions and components from this hobby are used in small civilian unmanned aircraft and their operation.

The use of unmanned aircraft by the military as targets for aerial gunnery practice and as reconnaissance platforms can be traced back to before the first world war. Initially, these aircraft employed rudimentary mechanical autopilots to maintain a single course and altitude but later RC systems were added in order to be able to control them remotely, albeit at short ranges. Eventually, small aircraft were outfitted with basic forms of memory and gyroscopes allowing them to execute simple commands or even be pre-programmed with flight plans while flying beyond the range of RC transmitters. Once launched, these aircraft would mindlessly "drone" along their predetermined flight path (perhaps snapping photos or impersonating an enemy plane along the way) until meeting their end in one form or another. This is the origin of the military *drone, an aircraft capable of autonomous flight but which cannot be monitored or controlled for most or all of its flight.* Similar principles of operation were later employed in the Nazi V weapons, the first guided ballistic missiles used to bombard England from Germany during WWII.

Drones continued to be used by the military for decades. However, technological advances—specifically increased computing power within a small space, greater data transmission capability, and the advent of the Global Positioning System (GPS)—allowed a similar but distinctly new type of aircraft to take on increasingly greater mission capabilities. Since their introduction into military service around the time of the first Persian Gulf War in the early 1990s, these aircraft have borne several technical acronyms, most notably unmanned air vehicle (UAV), but in the interest of brevity and demilitarization, we'll refer to them as **unmanned aircraft (UA).** *A UA may be piloted remotely, similar to an RC aircraft, or fly autonomously, like a drone, due to* *its distinguishing feature: an onboard flight controller with a two-way data transmission system. This system facilitates communication between the aircraft and a ground station, allowing an external pilot to both monitor the aircraft's status (i.e., position, altitude, heading) and send commands to the aircraft in flight.* Further technical advancements in the last decade have put these UAs within reach of the average person as their components become more widely available. These are the aircraft that will be discussed at length in this guide.

Recently, the term "drone" has become a catch-all for anything resembling the aircraft described above, regardless of actual configuration. This is especially true for multirotor airframes, the existence of which are due to the same recent advancements in technology that allow autonomous flight on a small scale. Moreover, for multiple reasons, multirotors have been many people's point of introduction into the world of RC and autonomous flight. The popularity of this term is partially due to the fact that "UAV" does not exactly roll off the tongue, and also because the imagery of flying robots roaming the skies of their own volition has been seized upon by some in the interest of sensationalism. Nevertheless, many experts and practitioners within the field, who in the past may have considered the term "drone" derogatory, seem to have yielded in their protests and begun to accept the term, at least in casual conversation.

The purpose of this text is to serve as a guide to the construction, operation, and maintenance of these small, electric UAs for both recreational and commercial use. Beginners in this field will be able to use this book as a point of entry, while more experienced operators will find ways to improve their systems and procedures. With UA technology readily available and huge commercial opportunities on the horizon, the objective of this book is to empower new operators with the knowledge required to use this technology safely, responsibly, and effectively.

Abbreviations

AC	alternating current		OSD	on-screen display
AGL	above ground level		PDB	power distribution board
ATC	air traffic control		PID	proportional-integral-derivative
BEC	battery eliminator circuit		PMU	power management unit
CG	center of gravity		PPM	pulse-position modulation
COA	certificate of waiver or authorization		PWM	pulse-width modulation
DC	direct current		RC	remote control
EDF	electric ducted fan		ROI	region of interest
ESC	electronic speed controller		RPC	remote pilot certificate
FAA	Federal Aviation Administration		RSSI	received signal strength indication
FPV	first-person view		RTH	return to home
GCS	ground control station		RX	receiver
GCU	gimbal control unit		TX	transmitter
GSD	ground sample distance		UA	unmanned aircraft
GPS	Global Positioning System		UAS	unmanned aircraft system
HUD	heads-up display		UAV	unmanned air vehicle
IMU	intertial measurement unit		UPS	uninterruptible power supply
IR	infrared		VFR	visual flight rules
LiPo	lithium polymer (battery)		VLOS	visual line-of-sight
LOS	line of sight		VTOL	vertical takeoff and landing
MUX	multiplexer			

CHAPTER ONE

Unmanned System Components

Ground Systems

UNMANNED AIRCRAFT SYSTEMS require a collection of ground-based components, which although not as glamorous as airborne components, are just as essential in order to operate safely and effectively. These components are commonly referred to together as a **ground control station (GCS)**. The elements of a GCS include an interface device, telemetry transceiver (combination transmitter/receiver), remote control (RC) transmitter, payload interface, and power sources.

Interface Device

The interface device is a means of displaying data received from the aircraft for monitoring flight status as well as command options for controlling the aircraft. In most cases, the interface device is a laptop, tablet, or mobile device running appropriate mission control software.

This software will usually be accompanied by the software drivers required to utilize the telemetry transceiver unit. The primary function of this software is twofold: to present telemetry data coming from the aircraft to the user and to allow the user to transmit commands to the aircraft. This mission control software may have a secondary purpose of configuring and maintaining the aircraft (for example, accessing system errors, troubleshooting vibration issues, or analyzing power consumption).

/ SELECTING A SYSTEM

When selecting an interface device, the first important consideration is ensuring it will support the mission control software, as not all of these software packages are agnostic to operating on all systems. Furthermore, it is essential to select a system suitable for the mission profile and operating environment in which it will be used. These considerations may lead to selecting a tablet over a traditional laptop. It can also be beneficial to select a device that is suitably ruggedized to meet the operating environment; otherwise, the device may require aftermarket ruggedization, including cases and screen protectors. As it may be necessary to input commands as quickly as possible, a touchscreen can be advantageous but may not completely replace a keyboard, and it may also lead to inadvertent inputs. Finally, in most cases it is preferable to choose an interface device with multiple USB ports, an HDMI port (or other means of externally displaying or expanding the screen imagery), and an SD card port for readily downloading camera images as required.

Telemetry Transceiver (TX/RX)

A transceiver, a combination of a telemetry transmitter and receiver, is a hardware module connected to a standard interface device allowing two-way wireless data transmission between the aircraft and the ground station.

Normally, telemetry transceiver units are specific to or dictated by the mission control software and/or flight controller system being used. The ground unit is typically identical to the air unit on the vehicle, although the external housing or casing of the air unit may be removed in order to reduce weight where prudent and possible.

In order to achieve the best possible signal between the GCS and the aircraft, it is important to provide the ground telemetry unit with the best possible "view" of the aircraft during flight. This is commonly done by elevating the unit (or its antenna), which may also serve to distance the unit from sources of interference. This may be accomplished simply by fixing the unit atop a telescoping pole mount. It is important to note that the practical maximum length of a low-speed USB cable is approximately 9 feet; therefore, it may be necessary to use Ethernet cabling and converters for certain applications.

Remote Control Transmitter (RC TX)

A **remote control transmitter** (**RC TX**) is the handheld ground component of the RC system and serves as the primary means of controlling the aircraft when it is not in an autonomous flight mode.

Certain mission control software packages have been developed and vetted to such a degree that RC systems are not necessarily required for normal operations. After all, the main benefit of unmanned systems is that they do not normally require the highly technical skill of RC flying. However, an RC transmitter in the hands of a competent pilot and assisted by the stabilization of the flight controller is a highly recommended insurance policy for professional operations and will likely be required by regulatory agencies in the near future. While RC transmitters initially can be intimidating, they provide a more direct means of interfacing with the aircraft and commanding flight and payload functions.

The RC transmitter system will be described in more detail in the "Remote Control Systems" section later in this chapter.

Payload Interface

The payload interface includes any additional equipment required to operate the aircraft's payload. For example, in a first-person view (FPV) video system, this would consist of a monitor and video receiver.

An example payload setup for such an FPV system is covered in detail in the Imaging Sensor Payloads section later in this chapter.

Power Sources

The GCS must have a system for providing reliable power to the electronic systems described above while operating in the field. This may consist of a combination of generators, auto battery and inverter, and spare system batteries.

Due to the dependence on power to continue safe flight operations, the following considerations and options are important in order to allow for redundant power supplies:

- All power supply options require an appropriate length of extension cord(s). One or two heavy-duty reels of 100 feet or more in length is advisable for most circumstances.

- It is recommended to have a LiPo battery charger available in the field.

- Use outlet power whenever possible. This requires appropriate circuit breakers or fuses in order to support the load.

- Small gas generators can provide several hours of power under normal circumstances. However, these generators can struggle under a heavy load, such as when powering multiple devices and/or charging batteries. They can also be dirty and noisy.

- DC-to-AC inverters running off automobile batteries may be used to power short-term, small-scale operations. However, special care should be taken not to fully discharge the battery.

- Ensure that you have spare batteries for ground components. It is often prudent to have at least two fully-charged batteries for each component, including the interface device, RC transmitter, and FPV monitors.

- An uninterruptible power supply (UPS) is a highly recommended backup power system that is capable of immediately providing power for several minutes in the event of main power system failure. This can facilitate a safe landing and shutdown in the event of a generator failure or blown fuse, for example. UPS systems are available in several forms, one of the most useful resembling a bulky surge protector providing multiple outlets. UPS systems will commonly emit a loud audible tone in the event that power input is no longer being received, signaling that flight operations should be safely ended.

Remote Control (RC) Systems

MANY SMALL UNMANNED SYSTEMS rely on components from the hobby world of **remote control (RC) aircraft**, including servos, speed controllers, and the RC system itself. The airborne component of the RC system receives the pilot's command via signals from the RC transmitter and outputs corresponding commands to the flight controller.

Theory of Operation

RC systems consist of a **receiver** (RC RX) installed on board the aircraft and a handheld **transmitter** (RC TX) on the ground, and these systems are the basis for RC flying. Current systems operate at a frequency of approximately 2.4 gigahertz (GHz) and advertise a range of approximately 1 statute mile along line-of-sight (LOS), but this range can be extended using external modules.

The signal from the RC transmitter to the RC receiver contains the RC transmitter's unique binding code (described later in this section) as well as command inputs for a given number of "channels." Each channel corresponds to an attribute of the aircraft, the position or degree of which can be controlled by the pilot. The most common signal protocol for an individual channel is referred to as pulse-width modulation (PWM), which usually ranges from a low value of about 1000 to a high value of approximately 2000 microseconds (μs). These values correspond to the duration of time that the pulse waves are held high (width of the pulse).

Almost all RC transmitters include two control sticks (tiny joysticks) which are arranged side by side and can each be moved in two directions (up and down, and left and right) to control the four main flight control channels (pitch, roll, yaw, and thrust) *(Figure 1-1)*. The remaining channels, if any, can be assigned to switches or knobs on the RC transmitter by the operator based on their needs. In RC flying, these extra channels would usually be assigned to control accessories like flaps or retractable landing gear, but on unmanned aircraft (UA), they can be used to control flight modes, emergency modes, or payload functions.

Each channel usually corresponds to an individual three-wire servo output port on the RC receiver module *(Figure 1-2)*. Each wire in the standard three-wire servo connector is color coded, usually in a series of yellow, red and black; orange, red, and brown; or white, red and black. The yellow, orange, or white wire carries the control signal for the connection, the red wire supplies power, and the black or brown wire provides the ground for the other two wires. In RC flying, the 5 volts (V) of power that the RC receiver requires to operate is usually supplied from an external battery or a **battery eliminator circuit** (BEC) incorporated into an **electronic speed controller**

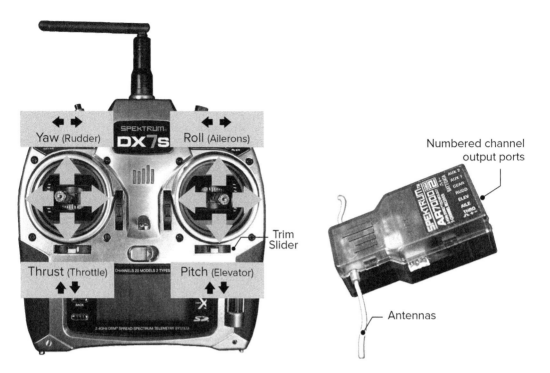

Figure 1-1. RC transmitter, mode 2 configuration.

Figure 1-2. RC receiver.

(**ESC**), which is connected to one of the output servo ports of the RC receiver. The RC receiver in turn shares this power with any other component connected to it (servos in most cases). In UA construction, however, the output ports of the RC receiver are connected to corresponding input ports on the flight controller and, in turn, most flight controllers will provide the RC receiver with power over this connection.

Some RC receivers, rather than having individual ports for each channel, have the ability to communicate multiple channels over a single three-wire connector. These systems, such as the Futaba S.BUS system, can reduce wiring clutter considerably by carrying all commands from the RC receiver to the flight controller on a single, three-wire connection.

Configuration

Most programmable RC transmitters will support multiple aircraft models or profiles, allowing a single RC transmitter to be used to control multiple aircraft, a key selling point for hobbyists with a garage full of RC projects. Since these aircraft will obviously have very different configurations, a model or a profile will include the following basic selections.

/ BINDING

A 2.4 GHz RC system allows an operator to "bind" or pair a receiver with a specific RC transmitter. This process usually involves pushing a button on the RC transmitter and/or RC receiver, or inserting a special plug into the receiver while powering on both systems within close proximity. When binding is performed properly, a RC receiver will only respond to command signals that include the unique binding code of the RC transmitter with which it is paired. A similar system is used in automobile keyless entry remotes: most of these remotes operate within the same frequency band but each car responds only to a unique code broadcast on that frequency by its corresponding remote. This binding protocol allows multiple RC aircraft to operate nearby without interfering with each other, unlike older RC systems. It also allows the installation of multiple RC receivers on a single aircraft to create a multiple operator system, which is the recommended configuration for large professional video aircraft with 3D gimbals (described in detail under Imaging Sensor Payloads later in this chapter). Under normal circumstances, the binding procedure only needs to be performed once, but it can be a good idea to install the RC receiver so it is easily accessible within the aircraft in the event that binding must be repeated.

/ REVERSE

Reverse simply changes the output of a given stick, switch, or knob position from high to low PWM, or vice versa. If a control surface is not deflecting in the correct direction, the applicable RC channel may be reversed in order to correct this, making control surface deflections an important part of aircraft setup, which will be discussed later.

/ TRIM

Trim is a means of adjusting the current PWM value output by a certain channel. For example, if the nose of an airplane is constantly dipping down and the pilot must keep pressure on the pitch control stick to keep the aircraft level, then trim could be used to adjust the PWM value output when the pitch stick is in the center or neutral position to one that would maintain level flight. A well-trimmed aircraft flying on a calm day will usually not require any input from the pilot to continue flying straight and level (in the case of a fixed-wing aircraft) or maintain a stable hover (in the case of a rotor-wing aircraft). Most RC transmitters will include trim sliders next to the two main control sticks to adjust trim in flight. However, if a flight controller is being used, then trimming is best performed through that system rather than through the RC transmitter.

/ SUBTRIM

Subtrim performs the same function as trim, but is considered a deeper layer of programming. Whereas trims are usually controlled by knobs on the RC transmitter, subtrims are usually edited within the aircraft transmitter model or profile. Once proper trims are determined through flight testing, these values may be applied to the subtrims. This will allow the trims to be set to zero so that they are less likely to be inadvertently changed or forgotten. From this point, the pilot may still use the trim slider knobs to make small adjustments based on payload and flying conditions. Subtrims may also be used to set control surfaces to the proper neutral positions when it is not possible to achieve this mechanically (which is preferable).

/ END POINT

The end point adjustment allows the operator to change the range of PWM values that are allowed on a given channel. For example, this may be used to limit the range of gimbal tilt. Some servos may be capable of providing more range of motion than the attached linkage or control surface, putting undue stress on the servo. In this case, limiting the end point of the servo can be used to prevent the servo from exceeding its safe range of motion.

/ MIXING

Mixing allows the positions of two sticks, switches, or knobs to control the output of a single channel. Traditionally, this was important in RC fixed-wing flight with flaps and in helicopter flight. In UA flight, mixing, along with end point configuration, will prove important in controlling the aircraft while in manual flight modes, as will be described further in Chapter 2 and Chapter 5.

/ FAILSAFE

Some high-end RC systems will include a **failsafe system**, which, in general, is *a means of protecting or attempting to save the aircraft in the event of an emergency or adverse event.* In the case of an RC system, a failsafe will cause the RC receiver to output preprogrammed channel values in the event that the signal from the RC transmitter is lost for a specific period of time. This may be due to the aircraft flying out of range or the RC transmitter losing power. Ideally, the failsafe channel settings would be those providing the greatest likelihood of a safe termination of the flight assuming that the pilot cannot regain control. For example, the best failsafe outputs for a fixed-wing aircraft would most likely involve cutting the throttle to idle and pitching for a gentle glide with wings level. These failsafe outputs must be predetermined by the operator and are usually saved when the RC receiver and RC transmitter bind to each other. While this can be a very useful feature for RC flying, it is important to configure an RC failsafe system so as not to interfere with the signal provided by the flight controller, which is usually much more advanced.

Selecting a System

The first feature to take note of when selecting an RC system is the number of channels. The practical minimum number of channels required for UA operations is six, four of which are reserved for the main flight controls, leaving at least two channels to control the flight mode and an accessory such as a camera trigger or gimbal tilt. Three-position switches are another important feature to look for as they offer more convenient control of UA flight modes.

The two main control sticks on RC transmitters are usually spring-loaded in the pitch, roll, and yaw axes so the sticks will return to center when released. The channel intended to control the throttle, usually one of the "up and down" axes, is often left without this feature, especially for fixed-wing aircraft, so the throttle can be set and maintained. RC transmitters with the throttle on the right are referred to as Mode 1 or Mode 3, and those with the throttle on the left are referred to as Mode 2 or Mode 4 (*Figure 1-3*).

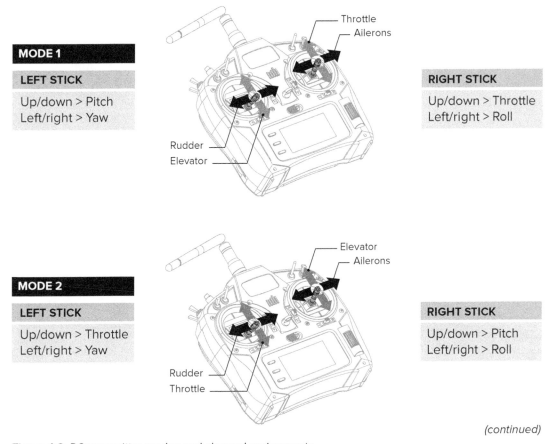

MODE 1

LEFT STICK
Up/down > Pitch
Left/right > Yaw

RIGHT STICK
Up/down > Throttle
Left/right > Roll

Throttle
Ailerons
Rudder
Elevator

MODE 2

LEFT STICK
Up/down > Throttle
Left/right > Yaw

RIGHT STICK
Up/down > Pitch
Left/right > Roll

Elevator
Ailerons
Rudder
Throttle

(continued)

Figure 1-3. RC transmitter modes and channel assignments.

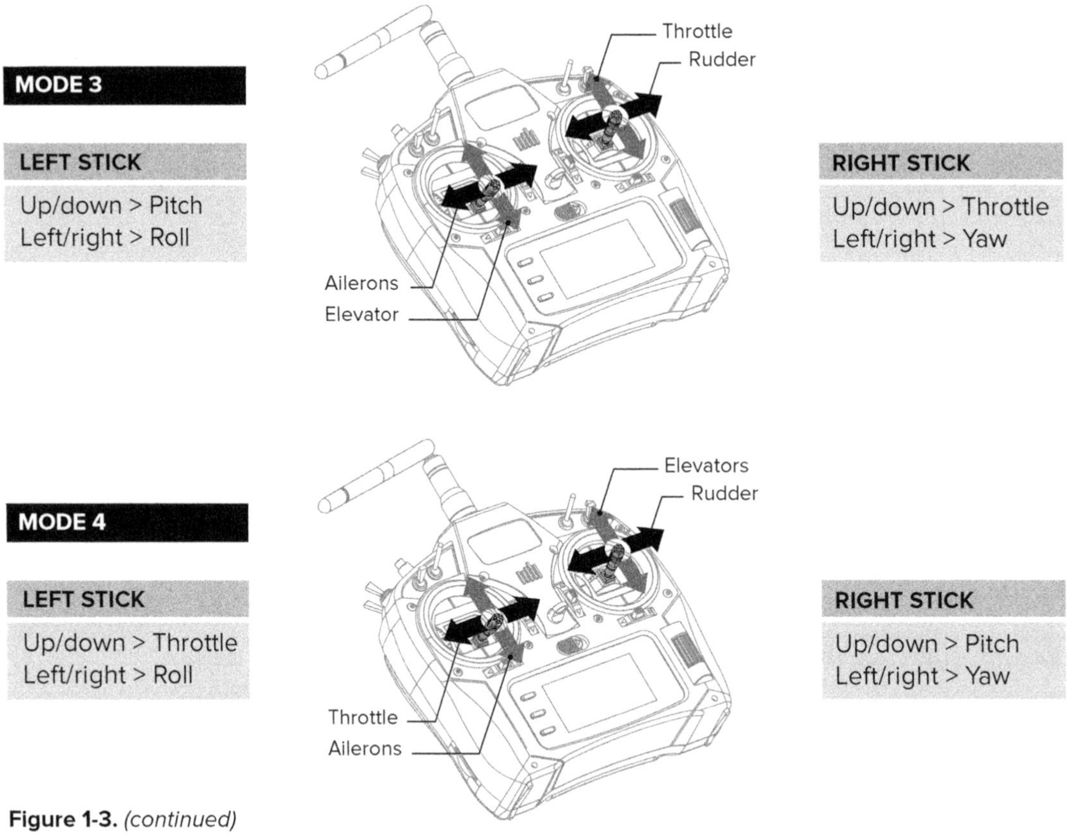

MODE 3

LEFT STICK

Up/down > Pitch
Left/right > Roll

Ailerons
Elevator

Throttle
Rudder

RIGHT STICK

Up/down > Throttle
Left/right > Yaw

MODE 4

LEFT STICK

Up/down > Throttle
Left/right > Roll

Throttle
Ailerons

Elevators
Rudder

RIGHT STICK

Up/down > Pitch
Left/right > Yaw

Figure 1-3. *(continued)*

Some RC transmitters include digital displays and inputs for configuring the system directly, which is much more convenient than having to connect the system to a laptop. Many of these RC transmitters also allow multiple aircraft profiles or models to be saved, allowing a single RC transmitter to be used to control multiple aircraft (but not at the same time). Some advanced RC systems will include failsafe and basic telemetry features; however, these are both usually disabled in favor of the systems offered by the flight controller.

An RC system with all of these features may turn out to be one of the more costly components within the overall UA system. However, the fact that it contributes directly to the safe flight of the aircraft, as well as the fact that the RC transmitter will remain intact even if the aircraft is completely lost, makes the RC system a good investment.

Some flight controllers allow video game controllers connected to a laptop to control the aircraft over the telemetry link in a similar fashion. While this can be a good idea in some cases, a better option may be an RC transmitter with a mounted video monitor and/or mobile device, which makes a great, self-contained, mobile means of controlling and monitoring the aircraft in the field.

Aircraft Systems

Introduction to Airframes

Three basic types of RC aircraft are readily available for adaptation as small unmanned aircraft. These aircraft can be divided into two categories based on their method of generating lift. Airplanes, which direct their thrust along their longitudinal axis in order to move through the air and derive lift from the air moving over their wings, are referred to as fixed-wing aircraft. Rotor-wing aircraft, including both traditional helicopters and multicopters, use a rotor or set of rotors to direct their thrust vertically in order to generate lift, and are thus considered capable of **vertical takeoff and landing** (**VTOL**). The VTOL capability and maneuverability afforded by rotor-wing aircraft allow them to operate well within small areas, while fixed-wing platforms offer significantly more endurance. Although they belong to separate categories, airplanes and helicopters both utilize movable control surfaces in order to effect maneuvers, while multicopters accomplish this electronically using ESCs. Table 1-1 shows a comparison of these airframe categories, including the pros, cons, and typical missions for each.

Table 1-1. Comparison of airframe categories

AIRPLANE	HELICOPTER	MULTICOPTER
Longitudinal thrust (fixed wing)	Vertical thrust (rotor wing)	
Physical control surfaces (servos)		Electronic RPM control (ESCs)
PROS		
- High endurance - Simple flight control - Low to moderate complexity - High failure tolerance (glide)	- High maneuverability - VTOL capability - Hover capability	- High maneuverability - VTOL and hover capability - Mechanically simple - Non-directional - Relatively low-cost - Compact, packable
CONS		
- Low maneuverability - Large operating area required	- Mechanically complex - Electronically complex - Low failure tolerance	- Electronically complex - Low endurance - Low failure tolerance
MISSIONS		
- High-altitude FPV - Persistent surveillance/data acquisition - Large area surveying - Cargo (air drop) - Harsh weather	- *Use of a traditional helicopter as a small unmanned aircraft is not recommended.*	- Low-altitude, close-proximity FPV - Small area surveying - Swarm or team operations - Pack-in - Cargo (touchdown)

/ MULTICOPTER THEORY

Multicopters consist of an arrangement of motors spinning attached propellers that are used to generate vertical lift. Airplanes can be seen as an elegant aerodynamic solution resembling flying animals in nature. Helicopters are more of a feat of human ingenuity but are still aerodynamically stable for the most part. Multicopters, on the other hand, use pure brute force and are based on the principle that if you strap enough motors to an object, it will fly. However, this arrangement is incredibly aerodynamically unstable and on its own would become uncontrollable before a human pilot would have time to intervene. Therefore, all multicopters require flight controllers in order to maintain stability by independently varying the speeds of each of the motors to produce maneuvers or maintain a level hover. Because multicopters have very few moving parts—in theory, only the motors and propellers—these aircraft are mechanically simple and can be very compact. While their high degree of electronic complexity translates to more potential points of failure, many of these are not outwardly apparent to the operator; out of sight, out of mind. On multicopters with fewer than eight motors, a single motor failure usually leads to a loss of the aircraft due to lack of control and lifting thrust.

Airframes

Multicopters come in a wide variety of airframe configurations. It is important to remember that multicopters are designed with a front only for the benefit of a human operator. In fact, almost all multicopters perform identically flying in any horizontal direction. In some cases (for example, flying autonomous grid survey missions), this provides multicopters with a distinct advantage over airplanes and helicopters by allowing sensors to be held in a constant orientation throughout the flight.

Quadcopters, Hexacopters, and Octocopters—The most common multicopter configurations have between four and eight arms radiating from a central hub with motor mounts on the outboard end of each arm. These airframes may have their forward direction oriented either along a single arm (usually the number 1 arm), which is commonly referred to as a "+" configuration, or between two arms (usually the number 1 and 2 arms), which is commonly referred to as an "X" configuration (*Figure 1-4*). Neither of these configurations has distinct advantages over the other.

On these airframes, each motor is set up to spin in the opposite direction as the adjacent motors. This balances the angular momentum of the system, which would otherwise cause the aircraft to spin if more propellers were spinning in one direction than the other.

Coaxial Motor Arrangements—Some airframes will allow motors to be mounted on both the top and bottom of the outboard motor mounts. The advantage of this coaxial arrangement is that a given number of motors require half as many arms, which can both significantly reduce the weight of the airframe and allow for a more compact airframe with less aerodynamic drag. Therefore, coaxial aircraft can be ideal for applications requiring high speeds, high lift capacity, and/or a small

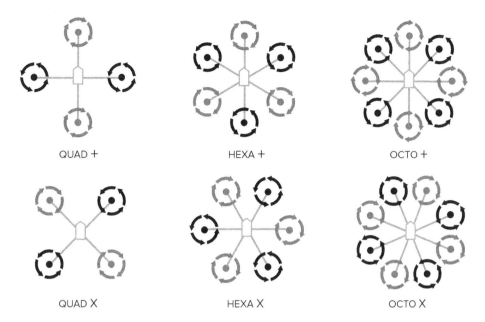

Figure 1-4. Quadcopters, hexacopters, and octocopters in both + and X configurations.

Figure 1-5. Y6 and X8 coaxial airframes.

Figure 1-6. I/H airframe configuration.

pack-down size. However, the coaxial arrangement of propellers tends to be less aerodynamically efficient compared to two propellers each encountering "clean," undisturbed airflow. The most common coaxial motor arrangements are the Y6 and X8 *(Figure 1-5)*.

I or H configurations—I or H configuration airframes have motor arrangements very similar to an X4 quadcopter, but they consist of two continuous booms with motor mounts at each outboard end *(Figure 1-6)*. These booms are secured to the front and rear of a central fuselage. These airframes usually provide ample mounting space on or in their central fuselage and many will have removable or folding booms, allowing for more compact transport. I and H airframe configurations usually lend themselves to quadcopters and coaxial octocopters.

Asymmetric Airframes—Asymmetric versions of airframes with X4–X8 motor arrangements are becoming more popular because they are visually distinctive. However, it is important to remember that the proper center of gravity location for a multicopter is at the center of the hypothetical circle of motors, which can be difficult to obtain with an off-center central hub *(Figure 1-7)*.

Figure 1-7. Asymmetric airframe.

Flight Maneuvers

A multicopter is capable of flying in a manner similar to a traditional helicopter, with the thrust from the propulsion system directed vertically, giving the aircraft the capability to hover. However, multicopters operate very differently than helicopters when it comes to producing maneuvers.

- *Climb and Descent*—A multicopter produces level climbs and descents simply by increasing or decreasing the RPM of all of the motors collectively. The balanced number of propellers spinning clockwise and counterclockwise will maintain a roughly constant heading. This is analogous to the collective pitch changes of a helicopter's main rotor blade.

- *Pitch and Roll*—Pitch and roll maneuvers are produced by increasing the RPM of motors on one side of the aircraft (increasing lift) while decreasing the RPM of the motors on the opposite side (decreasing lift). This will rotate the aircraft about either its lateral or longitudinal axis while attempting to maintain a roughly constant altitude. This is analogous to the cyclic pitch changes of a helicopter's main rotor blade.

- *Yaw*—Multicopter yaw maneuvers are slightly more complicated. In order to yaw to the right (clockwise), the flight controller will increase the RPM of all motors that are spinning counterclockwise while decreasing the RPM of those spinning clockwise. The airframe will react to the imbalance of counterclockwise angular momentum by rotating clockwise, to the right. Meanwhile, the arrangement of counter-rotating motors on alternating arms will keep the aircraft roughly level in spite of these RPM differences.

Motor Failure

As mentioned previously, a motor failure may be the result of a motor, ESC, or flight controller malfunction and will likely result in a rough landing or crash. The operator will likely observe an immediate descent caused by the decrease in lift and a wobbling yaw spiral or pirouette resulting from the imbalance in rotational energy. The fewer motors a multicopter has, the more pronounced these disturbances will be;

most quadcopters will be uncontrollable if a motor fails, while an octocopter may be capable of flying stably. But regardless of the multicopter configuration, in the case of a motor failure the aircraft should still land as soon as possible to avoid overstressing the flight controller and the remaining motors.

Selecting a Multicopter

When selecting a multicopter airframe, it is important to consider the following:

- *Number of Arms/Motors*—As a general rule, carrying any payload larger than a small camera like a GoPro demands at least six motors, both for lifting capacity and for greater redundancy in the event of a motor failure. However, these airframes tend to be less compact and portable. This makes coaxial motor arrangements especially appealing, with the added benefit of the reduced weight of fewer arms. One option to consider, especially if entertaining the possibility of expanding to larger payloads, is an airframe that allows for either single or coaxial mounting of motors. Such an airframe would allow, for example, a multicopter to begin flying as a quadcopter and then be upgraded to an octocopter at a later point, if necessary.

- *Motor and Propeller Compatibility*—It is important to verify that the motors selected can be mounted to the airframe and that the propeller size is appropriate (refer to the "Propulsion Systems" section later in this chapter).

- *Flight Controller, Battery, and Payload Mounting*—It is best to start planning the mounting of critical components before purchasing an airframe. Some airframes incorporate vibration-isolated payload rails and battery trays, which make the mounting of certain but not all types of payloads and batteries especially convenient. There is also the question of where to mount the flight controller, which would ideally be mounted where it is easily accessible. However, suitable locations for mounting the flight controller are often limited, especially on small aircraft, which usually require that the battery be mounted to the upper plate.

- *Retractable Landing Gear*—This feature might be important depending on the intended use for the multicopter. For example, when selecting an airframe for a professional cinematic video platform, retractable landing gear, or the ability to add them, can be essential for panning shots that might be blocked by fixed landing gear.

/ AIRPLANE THEORY

Although commonly known as airplanes, these are also referred to in technical parlance as **fixed-wing aircraft** because they generally are built around a single, non-rotating main wing. There are many variations, but a fixed-wing aircraft's most

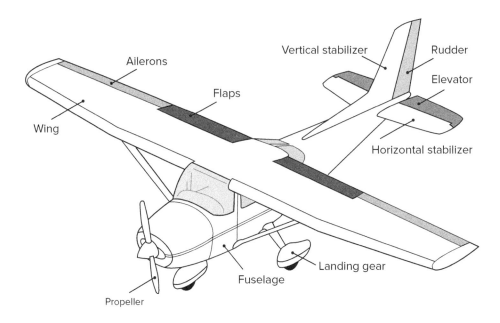

Figure 1-8. Airplane components.

basic form is comprised of a fuselage (or main body), a single wing passing through the fuselage, and an empennage (or tail), which usually includes both vertical and horizontal stabilizers *(Figure 1-8)*.

The Airfoil and the Wing

When viewed from an end or wing tip, the wing of an airplane has a distinctive, two-dimensional shape known as an **airfoil** *(Figure 1-9)*. The front of this airfoil is referred to as the leading edge and the rear is referred to as the trailing edge. The **chord line** is an imaginary line that bisects the airfoil, passing from the leading edge to the trailing edge. When the shape is extruded into a three-dimensional body, it forms a basic airplane wing. As a mass of moving air encounters the leading edge of this wing, it divides to pass both over and under the wing. The differences in curvature between the wing's upper and lower surfaces result in higher air pressure below the wing than above it. This pressure differential is observed as a net upward force on the wing; commonly known as **lift**, this is the force that allows powered flight. But as a byproduct of lift, the wing also generates **drag**, a force directed toward the rear of the wing. Drag can be thought of as the price of the wing's disturbance of the flow of air.

Generally, drag increases proportionally to lift, which may be altered by changing either the airflow around the wing (velocity) or the **angle of attack**—the angle between the direction of the moving air mass that encounters the wing and the chord line of that wing *(Figure 1-9)*. The angle of attack is related to the pitch of the aircraft

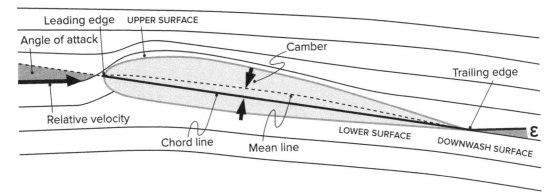

Figure 1-9. An example of an airfoil (viewed from wing tip).

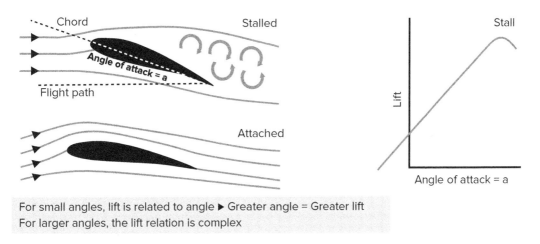

For small angles, lift is related to angle ▶ Greater angle = Greater lift
For larger angles, the lift relation is complex

Figure 1-10. Angle of attack, lift, and stall. (*NASA*)

but is not necessarily the same. As the angle of attack is increased, the wing will generate both more lift and more drag. This increase in lift only occurs up to a distinct point, because as the angle of attack increases, airflow around the wing becomes more disturbed, manifesting in increased drag. Because lift is dependent on the smooth flow of air around the curves of the wing, at a specific angle of attack the wing will no longer be capable of generating lift, resulting in a condition referred to as a **stall** (*Figure 1-10*). The risk of a stall is highest at low speeds when there is not enough airflow around the wing to generate the lift required to counteract the weight of the aircraft. In addition, stalls are especially dangerous at low altitude where there is less chance (or time) for recovery, making takeoff and landing particularly hazardous.

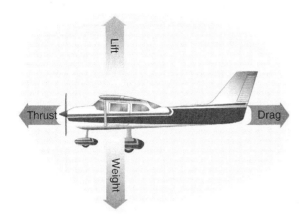

Figure 1-11. The four forces.

The Four Forces

An airplane in flight is constantly under the influence of four competing forces: lift, thrust, drag, and weight *(Figure 1-11)*.

As discussed in the previous section, lift is the product of the wing allowing the aircraft to counteract the opposite force, weight, and leave the Earth's surface. However, in the case of airplanes, this lift is dependent on the forward movement of the aircraft through the air to produce airflow around the wings. This forward movement is the result of **thrust**, the force generated by the propulsion system through a propeller or turbine, which allows the aircraft to accelerate and maintain constant velocity, counteracting drag. Gliders are the notable exception: with no onboard propulsion system, these aircraft convert potential energy (altitude) gained through various external means (tow plane, launcher, the natural rise of warm air, etc.) into kinetic energy (velocity) as a substitute for thrust. As previously discussed, drag is a byproduct of lift, but it may also result from friction or air resistance caused by any part of the airplane moving through the air.

Lift and thrust may be controlled, in a sense, directly by the pilot, but these forces have a complex relationship with the other two forces—weight and drag. For example, an increase in throttle setting will directly result in forward acceleration and an increase in velocity, which will likely also result in more airflow around the wing and greater lift—and, in turn, greater drag. Similarly, a change in pitch of the aircraft will result in a change in airspeed as well as a change in angle of attack, lift, and drag. When the four forces are balanced, the aircraft is said to be in straight-and-level, unaccelerated flight. This is the state a pilot or an autopilot will attempt to maintain during most flight operations.

Control Surfaces and Flaps

Airplanes maneuver through the use of **control surfaces**, which consist of movable panels located on the trailing edges of the tail and outboard sections of the wing, collectively referred to as aerodynamic surfaces. These control surfaces operate on the principle that the angle between the chord line of the aerodynamic surface and the flight direction (the angle of attack) can be altered (increased or decreased) in order to increase or decrease the lift produced by that surface and rotate the aircraft about its three major axes. Primary flight control surfaces include the rudder, ailerons, and elevators, while flaps are considered secondary flight controls as they are usually only deployed during takeoff and landing *(Figure 1-8)*.

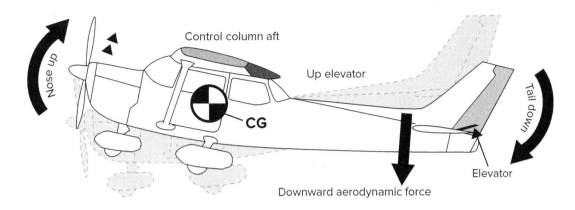

Figure 1-12. The location and operation of the elevator.

Elevators—These control surfaces on the horizontal stabilizer may be deflected downward in order to produce more lift on that aerodynamic surface, rotating the tail upward and the nose downward. Deflecting the elevators upward will result in negative lift or a downforce on the horizontal tail, pointing the nose upward *(Figure 1-12)*. This control surface is responsible for changes in pitch, rotating the aircraft about the lateral axis.

Rudder—Similarly, the control surface referred to as the rudder on the vertical stabilizer may be deflected either left or right in order to generate a side force in the opposite direction, thus yawing the aircraft *(Figure 1-13)*. This force generated by the rudder rotates the aircraft about the vertical axis. The rudder is primarily used to coordinate the aircraft when banking or turning.

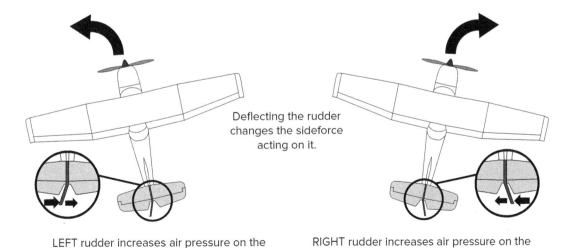

Figure 1-13. The location and operation of the rudder.

Ailerons—A pair of control surfaces called ailerons located near the wing tips deflect oppositely from one another to produce changes in roll (rotation of the aircraft about the longitudinal axis). For example, if a right roll is commanded, the right aileron will deflect upward, decreasing lift or creating a downward force on that wing tip, forcing it to lower. At the same time, the left aileron will lower, producing more lift on that wing tip and raising it up to produce the desired right roll *(Figure 1-14)*.

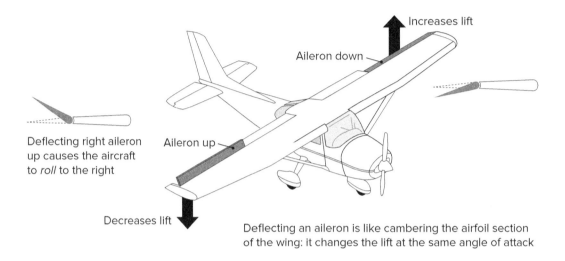

Increases lift

Aileron down

Deflecting right aileron up causes the aircraft to *roll* to the right

Aileron up

Decreases lift

Deflecting an aileron is like cambering the airfoil section of the wing: it changes the lift at the same angle of attack

Figure 1-14. The location and operation of the ailerons.

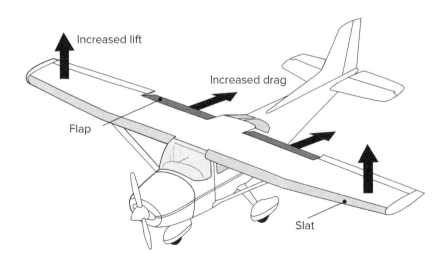

Increased lift

Increased drag

Flap

Slat

Figure 1-15. The location and function of flaps.

Flaps—Some airplanes incorporate flaps, which are similar to control surfaces in operation and principle and are considered secondary flight controls. Flaps consist of movable panels on the trailing edges of the wings, usually inboard of the ailerons on either side of the fuselage *(Figure 1-15)*. Both flaps are deflected downward together in order to increase the angle of attack of a large section of the wings without changing the pitch of the aircraft, thus generating greater lift at a given airspeed. With an increase in lift, the aircraft will be able to fly at a slower airspeed without the danger of stalling and achieve greater descent angles without a proportional increase in airspeed. Therefore, flaps are primarily useful during takeoff and landing, allowing for shorter takeoff runs and safer slow flight for approach to landing. The tradeoff, however, is that the deployment of the flaps results in much higher drag, both from increased lift and from the air resistance of the flaps themselves.

Coordination of Turns

A fixed-wing aircraft turns by banking, meaning it rolls its wing tip down in the direction of the turn. This redirects the lift vector, which is always perpendicular to the wingspan, in the direction of the intended turn and pulls the aircraft into a circular turn. However, because the magnitude of the lift vector is constant for a given airspeed, banking the aircraft reduces the vertical (opposing gravity) component of the lift. Thus an aircraft in a banking turn and at a constant throttle setting will require the generation of more lift, achieved by increasing pitch, in order to maintain a constant altitude *(Figure 1-16)*.

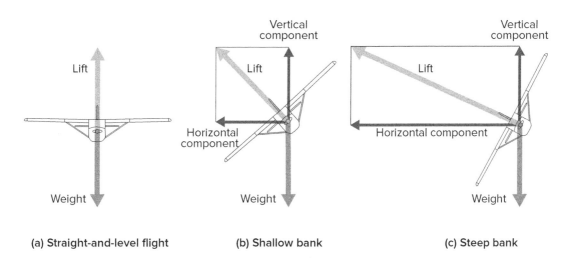

Figure 1-16. Lift vector in a banking turn: To maintain a constant altitude as the bank angle increases, the total lift vector must increase to keep the vertical component of lift equal to the weight.

Wing and Tail Variations

Fixed-wing aircraft come in a wide range of configurations, mainly distinguished by variations in the wings *(Figure 1-17)* and tail *(Figure 1-18)*.

- *Straight Wing*—The simplest, most traditional wing variation is a straight wing with a generally rectangular profile *(Figure 1-17A–D)*. Straight wings, especially with greater wingspans (the distance between wing tips), provide greater lift, even at lower speeds, and are best used on vehicles carrying greater payloads or intended for high endurance. Straight wings with a consistent airfoil profile across their span are sometimes referred to as "Hershey Bar wings" in the RC world.

- *Swept Wings*—Wings with the swept leading edge wing profile generally have reduced wingspans when compared to straight wings *(Figure 1-17E)*. This reduces drag and favors high-speed flight but will reduce low-speed performance.

- *Delta Wing*—Delta wings also have a swept leading edge while combining the surface of the wing and the fuselage, making the entire aircraft a single lifting body *(Figure 1-17F)*. These aircraft usually forgo vertical and horizontal tails in favor of two control surfaces on the wings acting as both ailerons and elevators (commonly referred to as elevons). This configuration does require the two-servo aileron configuration and elevon mixing but generally makes the aircraft mechanically simpler, with fewer points of failure. Delta-wing aircraft are usually fairly robust, having a single continuous body, and they can provide ample internal

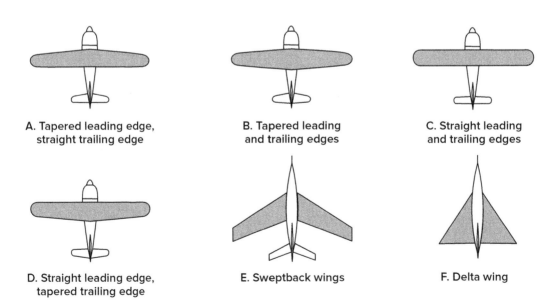

A. Tapered leading edge, straight trailing edge

B. Tapered leading and trailing edges

C. Straight leading and trailing edges

D. Straight leading edge, tapered trailing edge

E. Sweptback wings

F. Delta wing

Figure 1-17. Airplane wing configurations.

space depending on the model. However, in most cases these aircraft have rear-mounted or pusher propellers (instead of the conventional idea of an airplane with a front-mounted or tractor propeller), which can make them difficult or even dangerous to hand launch. If these aircraft do not incorporate a vertical tail, as many do not, they may also suffer from diminished yaw control.

- *Standard Tail*—The standard and most common tail configuration is the fuselage-mounted tail, with the horizontal tail below the vertical tail and intersecting at the fuselage *(Figure 1-18A)*. This type of empennage configuration is common among RC airplanes, as it tends to provide simple and strong construction along with straightforward control.

- *T-Tail*—A T-tail can be described as a horizontal tail mounted on top of a vertical tail *(Figure 1-18B)*. While this configuration can remove the horizontal tail from the turbulent prop wash created by a propeller, T-tails can be fragile and difficult to integrate mechanically.

- *V-Tail*—V-tails incorporate two diagonally mounted tails in place of the horizontal and vertical tails *(Figure 1-18C)*. V-tails can reduce the amount of material used in the empennage, reducing the aircraft weight and shifting the center of gravity (CG) forward. However, these empennages do require special mixing and can introduce unwanted roll when attempting to yaw.

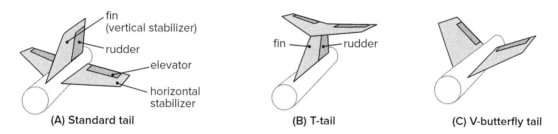

Figure 1-18. Airplane tail configurations.

Servo Configurations

RC airplanes tend to resemble their larger manned counterparts. In most cases, a single servo is responsible for moving each individual control surface. However, there are some notable exceptions, which are described in the following sections.

Straight and Swept Wing Ailerons—In some small airplanes, a single centrally mounted servo, along with a V-shaped control rod arrangement, controls both ailerons *(Figure 1-19)*. With the control surface horns and rods usually affixed to the underside of the ailerons, the rotating of the servo will pull on one rod to move that aileron down, while simultaneously pushing on the opposite rod to move the other aileron up.

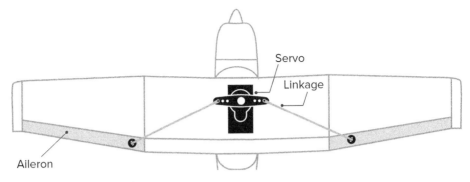

Figure 1-19. Single servo aileron control.

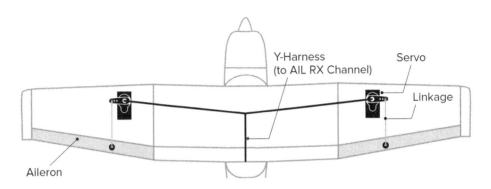

Figure 1-20. Two-servo aileron control.

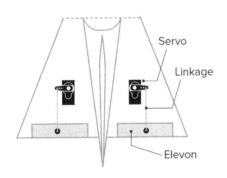

Figure 1-21. Delta wing servo configuration.

In larger aircraft with the ailerons separated by a greater distance, when the wings are separate and detachable, or when the wings incorporate flaps, two servos may be required—one to control each aileron. In most cases, these servos are mounted in such a way that when they receive an identical PWM signal from the RC receiver, they will move the ailerons in opposite directions. This allows a single RC receiver channel to control both ailerons through a servo splitter cable or Y-harness *(Figure 1-20)*. However, in some cases each aileron servo may require its own RC receiver channel.

Delta Wing Ailerons—Since each control surface on the wing of a delta-wing aircraft acts as both an aileron and an elevator, it is easy to understand why each would need to act independently of the other and thus be controlled by a separate servo and separate RC receiver channel *(Figure 1-21)*. These channels must be appropriately mixed to control roll and pitch simultaneously.

V-Tail—Similar to the delta wing configuration, both V-tail control surfaces must be capable of moving independently to control pitch and yaw simultaneously, thus requiring two separate servos and RC receiver channels that are appropriately mixed (*Figure 1-22*).

Flaps—Flaps are located on the inboard section of the wing, near the fuselage. This potentially allows them to be controlled by a single, centrally-mounted servo on single-piece wings (*Figure 1-23*). In this case, when flaps are deployed, the servo will pull forward on two control rods simultaneously, moving both flaps downward.

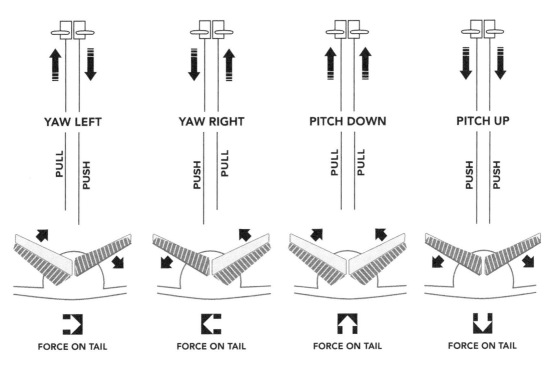

Figure 1-22. V-tail control.

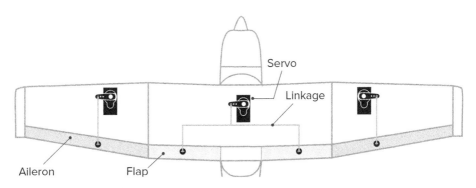

Figure 1-23. Single servo flap control.

On larger and separately removable wings, two servos may be required, one to control each flap *(Figure 1-24)*. In contrast to the two-servo aileron control configuration described previously, these flaps' servos are normally mounted so that if they receive an identical PWM signal from the RC receiver, the servos will move their corresponding flaps in the same direction, either extending them both down or retracting them both up. This allows a single RC receiver channel to control both ailerons through a servo splitter cable or Y-harness. However, in some cases each aileron servo may require its own RC receiver channel.

Nose/Tail Wheel—In both manned and RC airplanes, steering while moving on the ground (referred to as taxiing) is linked to the rudder. There are two common landing gear configurations: (1) Tricycle type, which incorporates a movable nose wheel and two, larger main gear and (2) Taildragger type, which incorporates a movable tail wheel and two, larger main gear *(Figure 1-25)*.

On taildragger aircraft, the tail wheel is usually either physically attached or mechanically linked to the rudder itself so that a single servo can be used to move both. On tricycle-type aircraft, the nose wheel may be controlled either by a single servo that moves two control rods (one linked to the rudder and the other linked to the nose wheel) or by two separate servos controlled by a single RC receiver channel through a Y-harness.

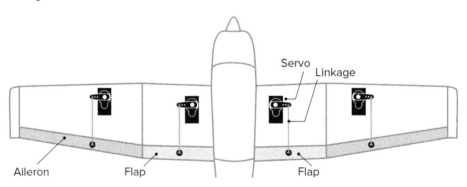

Figure 1-24. Two-servo flap control.

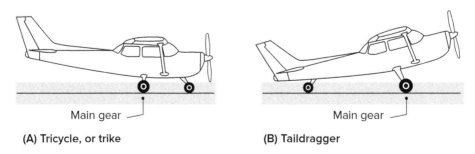

(A) Tricycle, or trike   **(B) Taildragger**

Figure 1-25. The two types of landing gear arrangements: (A) tricycle and (B) taildragger.

Landing gear—whether fixed, steerable, and/or retractable—are not usually practical for autonomous operations as they add weight and complexity to the system and also limit landing areas to long, smooth surfaces akin to a runway.

RC Setup

In most cases, the default channel and stick assignments for the RC transmitter in an airplane configuration are as shown in Table 1-2 and Figure 1-26. However, in most RC transmitters, these assignments may be altered as necessary (for example, to allow better left-handed control).

Table 1-2. Default RC Transmitter Channel and Stick Assignments (Mode 2)

CHANNEL	CONTROL SURFACE	MANEUVER	STICK/AXIS
1	Aileron	Roll	Right / Left-Right Axis
2	Elevator	Pitch	Right / Up-Down Axis
3	Throttle	Thrust	Left / Up-Down Axis
4	Rudder	Yaw	Left / Left-Right Axis

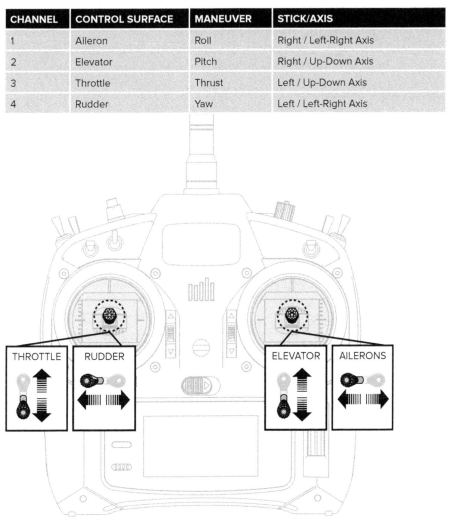

Figure 1-26. Default Mode 2 RC transmitter channel assignments.

Multiplexer

A **multiplexer** (**MUX**) is essentially a switch that can be installed on board an aircraft to allow the pilot to select between two sets of control inputs. When properly implemented, a MUX with at least four channels is wired between the flight controller and the maneuvering controllers. The MUX is also wired to receive inputs directly from the RC receiver. The pilot is then able to select between the signals coming from the flight controller, giving it authority over the flight of the aircraft, or those coming from the RC receiver, giving the pilot direct authority over the aircraft. Only the selected set of signals is passed through the MUX to the maneuvering controllers. MUXs do require a very specific setup to allow for effective switching between authorities, but they are highly recommended for fixed-wing aircraft.

Selecting an RC Airplane

When selecting an RC airplane, important considerations include internal space, launch capability, recovery method, construction material, and RC-specific components.

- *Internal Space*—It is important to ensure that ample internal space exists for all of the necessary RC equipment, the battery, the flight controller and its peripherals, and the payload while staying within the weight and center of gravity (CG) limitations of the aircraft. It is also important to consider how these components will be accessed during regular maintenance.

- *Launch Capability*—The simplest way to launch a light aircraft is throwing it by hand. This method allows for launch almost anywhere. However, hand launching becomes very difficult when a heavy payload is added, and it can also be very dangerous if the aircraft has a pusher propeller configuration (unless the motor is mounted within a pod on the upper side of the aircraft). One alternative method is to use a launcher, which is more reliable for heavier aircraft and, if used properly, can also be safer. On the other hand, a launcher adds a heavy, bulky component to the ground support equipment. Use of traditional, wheeled landing gear is the least practical for autonomous operations because most missions are conducted from small, uneven, and austere areas. Landing gear also adds weight to the system, and if the gear is not retractable, increases drag.

- *Recovery Method*—In most cases, the best recovery method for an autonomous vehicle is a belly landing, with replaceable, sacrificial skid material on the underside of the aircraft if necessary. (Packing tape is a cheap and easy solution.) However, this method may risk damage to certain components, such as the lens of a down-facing camera. Once again, the use of traditional, wheeled landing gear is less practical, requiring a precise landing approach and a long flat landing area. Devices such as nets and tail-hook cables may be used to decrease the ground run of the aircraft, but they also require time-consuming set-up and add weight and bulk to the ground support equipment.

- *Material*—There is some resistance in the professional small UAV community to the use of foam in airplanes, mostly among those in sales rather than engineering. In reality, foam is cheaper, lighter, and easier to repair than other common materials like plastic, wood, and composites. Foam is also easily cut (especially using a hot knife) to allow for mounting of components and routing of wires. Coatings and foam-safe paint may be used to improve the appearance and resilience of a foam aircraft, and foam repair materials (like sandable filler) can be found at hobby shops and hardware stores. If in doubt, customers tend to place more importance on the aircraft's ability to complete its mission, provide relevant data, and operate cost-effectively than on the aircraft's appearance.

- *Specific RC Components*—It is easy to be tempted by specific RC components such as electronic ducted fans (EDFs) and retractable landing gear. However, these systems are better suited for scale warbirds built for fun than for autonomous aircraft. EDFs are notoriously inefficient and have a nasty habit of ingesting foreign objects, resulting in costly repairs. Propellers, on the other hand, are cheaper and easier to replace. It is true that retractable landing gear can reduce drag and improve lifting efficiency, but they also add substantial weight and complexity to the system. As previously discussed, it is often better not to use landing gear than to use retractable, unless they are absolutely necessary.

/ HELICOPTER THEORY

Many people are familiar with the concept of a traditional helicopter, but very few not involved in operating them have a real appreciation for the marvel of how they work. At the most basic level, large main rotor blades with airfoil cross sections generate lift as they spin through the air, driven by the motor through a drive shaft. However, the application is not quite that simple. An incredibly complex device called a **swash plate** is used to vary the pitch, and therefore the **angle of attack**, of the main rotor blades throughout their rotation. Responding to control inputs of the pilot, the swash plate can be used to increase or decrease the lift generated by the main rotor as a whole, referred to as a **collective maneuver**, which is used to climb or descend. The swash plate is also capable of altering the pitch of individual blades, which is referred to as a **cyclic maneuver** and is used to tilt the arc of the main rotor, tilting its lift vector and maneuvering the aircraft in pitch and roll. The spinning main rotor contains an immense amount of rotational energy, and most helicopters employ a tail rotor to counter this energy and prevent it from causing the main body of the helicopter to rotate in the opposite direction. A tail rotor is composed of a smaller set of blades mounted at the rear of the aircraft on the end of a tail boom, which contains either a drive or belt to direct energy from the motor. The tail rotor is oriented so that the side force it generates (lift, but directed to the side rather than upward) counters the angular momentum of the main rotors. Meanwhile, a simplified swash plate is used to alter the pitch of the tail rotor blades collectively, varying the magnitude of the side force that is generated and allowing the pilot to control the yaw of the aircraft (*Figure 1-27*).

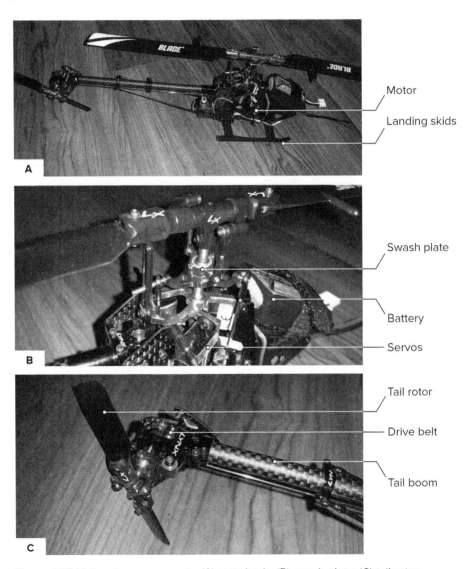

Motor

Landing skids

Swash plate

Battery

Servos

Tail rotor

Drive belt

Tail boom

Figure 1-27. Helicopter components: (A) main body; (B) swash plate; (C) tail rotor.

The Case against Helicopters as Autonomous Platforms

Traditional helicopters are the least-used airframes for small unmanned aircraft. Having addressed the theory behind these systems, we can see some of the reasons why they lack in popularity:

- The mechanics discussed in the previous section require many small, moving, interacting parts that are all subjected to constant vibrations in flight. When these parts are scaled down in size in an RC helicopter, it becomes clear why they can be a pain to work with. But in fact, helicopters tend to be maintenance nightmares regardless of their size. It is not uncommon to encounter military personnel who describe surviving multiple helicopter crashes, as if it is something that happens regularly. These factors can also make helicopter airframes and replacement parts cost-prohibitive.

- Helicopters are notoriously difficult to fly, requiring precise coordination of collective, cyclic, and yaw (leading RC helicopter pilots to tell you they are the best, often without being asked).

- They are perhaps the most dangerous of all RC platforms, comprised of what could be considered a pair of carbon fiber swords spinning at high RPM. This can be nerve-racking to say the least.

- The majority of RC helicopter airframes are currently designed for aerobatic flight rather than endurance. Therefore, multicopters are capable of delivering a longer endurance with a given payload while also operating more safely and reliably than helicopters of a similar size.

- At least at the time of this publication, very few flight controllers capable of autonomous flight are designed to support traditional helicopters.

- Almost all RC helicopter airframes currently available are constructed out of carbon fiber, which can severely interfere with signals to and from the aircraft.

- With the long main rotor overhead, there are no good locations on the airframe to mount the necessary GPS unit so that it will have a clear view of the sky.

For these reasons, the use of a helicopter as an autonomous platform is not recommended, especially for beginners. That is not to say that building an autonomous system from an RC helicopter is impossible, but it usually requires the use of a gas engine and a depth of helicopter experience.

Electrical System

/ POWER MANAGEMENT UNIT (PMU)

Power management units (PMUs) are generally external modules specific to a flight controller system that supply power to components from the main battery. The PMU usually has three leads or connectors, the first of which connects directly to the flight battery and leads to the main PMU circuit board. This lead is the connection point where the operator will attach the flight battery in order to power on the aircraft. The PMU circuit board regulates the power supplied to the flight controller through a second connector, since many flight controllers operate at a specific voltage that is lower than that of most flight batteries. Finally, a third connector supplies the voltage of the flight battery to motors and other electrical components, just as in an RC aircraft without a flight controller. Some PMUs are capable of monitoring the power draw of these systems and providing this data to the flight controller. Most PMUs are capable of supplying power to the main flight controller board, any connected sensors, the RC receiver, and the telemetry unit, but will not power servos or actuators connected to the flight controller. It is important to understand the voltage limits of the PMU, which are usually expressed in terms of LiPo battery cell count, before connecting to power.

/ POWER DISTRIBUTION BOARD (PDB)

A power distribution board (PDB) serves the relatively simple yet important purpose of supplying the voltage of the flight battery to the many components on the aircraft *(Figure 1-28)*. The most common use of a PDB is to provide power to the many ESCs, and in turn motors, on a multicopter aircraft. However, PDBs can be very useful on aircraft with many components requiring the voltage of the flight battery to operate. PDBs are generally arranged into pairs of positive (+, red) and negative/ground (−, black) output terminals, each intended to supply the voltage of the flight battery to a separate component. These terminals may come soldered with bullet connectors, which are very useful as they allow components to be easily removed and replaced without requiring desoldering. Some PDBs will also include a separate pair of terminals for input of flight battery power, which, in autonomous aircraft, is to be connected to the high-voltage power output of the PMU. Even on multicopters, it is a good idea

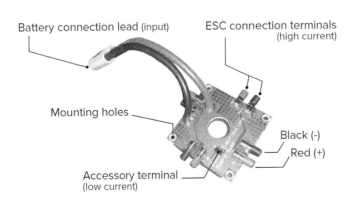

Battery connection lead (input)

ESC connection terminals (high current)

Mounting holes

Black (-)

Red (+)

Accessory terminal (low current)

Figure 1-28. Power distribution board (PDB).

to select a PDB with more output terminals than motors to allow extra terminals for other components. Be aware that some components will require lower voltage than that of the flight battery, and these components could be damaged by the application of higher voltage, thus requiring the use of a BEC (explained in more detail in the following section). It is also important to understand that PDBs, as the hub of high-voltage energy on the aircraft, are often one of the strongest sources of interference on aircraft; therefore, sensitive components, such as the GPS/compass module, should be physically separated or otherwise insulated from the PDB.

/ BATTERY ELIMINATOR CIRCUIT (BEC)

Battery eliminator circuits (**BECs**), also known as voltage regulators, generally accept the input of the flight battery voltage and output a lower voltage to components that require it. These BECs come in various forms and serve many purposes. In the beginning of RC flying, when almost all aircraft were gas powered, a small, low-voltage battery was required to power the onboard electrical components. These batteries served the same purpose as a motor-driven generator on a manned aircraft and were connected to the RC receiver, which incorporated a common power and ground rail of connector pins. This meant that once the battery was connected, the RC receiver as well as any servos connected to it would be supplied with power. With the advent of electric motor aircraft, which generally require higher-voltage power supplies, RC pilots did not want to have to weigh down their aircraft with two separate batteries or charge and maintain these different batteries for flight. Therefore, because all brushless motors required an ESC that was connected to both the RC receiver and the flight battery, some ESCs incorporated circuitry that would step down the flight battery voltage to that required to operate the RC components and supply it to the receiver via the three-wire servo connector *(Figure 1-29)*. Thus, the need for a separate low-voltage battery was eliminated (explaining the origin of the term "battery eliminator circuit").

With LiPo batteries supplying higher voltage on aircraft, as well as the prevalence of components operating at different voltages, separate BECs have become very useful when building autonomous aircraft. In fact, the flight controller PMU is essentially a BEC combined with a battery monitor. Some of these separate BECs can be programmed to a specific output voltage, while others are fixed. Common uses for

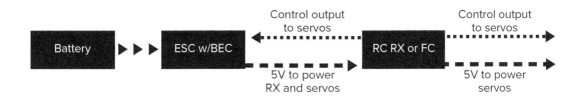

Figure 1-29. Internal battery eliminator circuit (BEC) implementation (airplane).

separate BECs include supplying power to video transmitters, lights, board cameras, camera triggers, and servos on multicopters. *It is important to note that BECs support only certain combinations of flight battery input voltage and the number of servos and ESCs connected to the system.* Higher-capacity BECs are referred to as universal BECs (UBECs) or switching BECs (SBECs).

/ LIPO BATTERIES

Lithium polymer (LiPo) batteries have become the power source of choice for small drone operators because of their high power density and discharge capability. However, these batteries require special consideration and care. LiPo batteries are distinguished by the following:

- *Cell Count and Arrangement*—LiPo batteries consist of multiple cells. The number of these cells arranged in series determines the fully charged voltage of the battery.

- *Capacity*—The capacity of LiPo batteries is most commonly rated in milliampere (milliamp) hours (mAh). For example, a battery rated for 2000 mAh (which is just a fancy way of saying 2 amp hours) will supply a current of 2 amps for approximately 1 hour before being fully discharged. Because straight-and-level flight in calm air requires an approximately constant current draw from the battery, the capacity of a battery is related to the flight time of the aircraft. All other things being equal, a LiPo battery with a higher mAh rating will provide a longer flight time, although not proportionally, as capacity also relates directly to the weight of the battery.

- *Discharge Rating*—The discharge rating or C-rating of the battery determines how much current (amps) may be safely drawn from the battery. If we consider the battery from the previous example, a 2000 mAh capacity with a C-rating of 10 would allow a maximum current draw of up to 20 amps, in which case the battery would last for approximately 6 minutes. It is important to pay careful attention to the C-rating when purchasing a battery, as some manufacturers will mark a battery with a so-called "maximum" C-rating that may be sustained for a few seconds, but the battery could be damaged if the lower "constant" C-rating is exceeded for too long. Some batteries will also be marked with a separate charging C-rating representing how much current can be safely supplied to the battery while charging to complete the process faster.

LiPo batteries can also be identified by two separate connectors: a discharge connector and a balance connector *(Figure 1-30)*.

A discharge connector lead usually consists of two, thick-gauge cables—one for power (red) and one for ground (black). This connector is used to supply the full voltage of the battery cell arrangement to the aircraft.

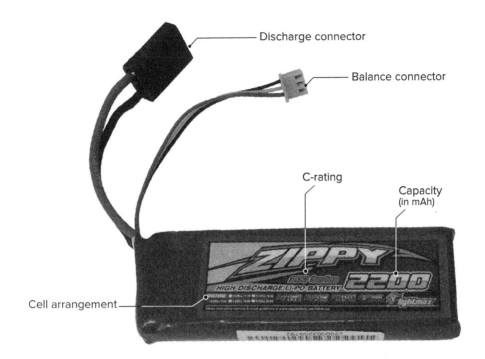

Discharge connector

Balance connector

C-rating

Capacity
(in mAh)

Cell arrangement

Figure 1-30. Lithium polymer (LiPo) battery. *(LIPO zippy 7.4V 2200mah; KundaliniZero;*
https://commons.wikimedia.org/wiki/File:LIPO_zippy.JPG; CC BY-SA 3.0)

A balance connector usually consists of multiple, thin-gauge cables. This
connector is used specifically for balance charging. This allows the charger to interface
with each cell separately and maintain balanced voltage across the cells. A balance lead
will have one more cable than the number of cells in series within the battery. This
lead may also be used with handheld battery cell checkers.

LiPo Battery Cells

LiPo batteries are made up of multiple cells containing the lithium polymer, and each
cell is limited to a specific voltage range regardless of physical size. These cells have
a nominal voltage of 3.7 volts but can be charged to a maximum voltage of 4.2 volts.
LiPo cells must not be discharged below an absolute minimum voltage of 3 volts,
otherwise the cell and the battery could be permanently damaged.

LiPo cells are now most commonly arranged in series within a battery; however,
some older battery packs may also have cells arranged in parallel. This arrangement is
usually abbreviated on the battery label in terms of the number of cells in series (S),
which form a branch of cells, and the number of these branches in parallel (P). For
example, a 3S2P battery would contain 6 cells: 2 parallel branches each consisting of 3
cells in series. If there is no P in the abbreviation, then the battery only consists of cells
arranged in series. Thus the abbreviation 4S is the equivalent of 4S1P *(Figure 1-31)*.

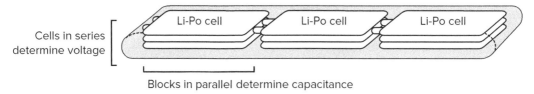

Figure 1-31. LiPo battery cell arrangement.

In early LiPo batteries, parallel arrangements of cells were used to increase the overall capacity of the battery packs, thus increasing the length of time these batteries could supply a constant voltage, generally equating to longer flight time. However, with better battery chemistry, this now is accomplished with physically larger cells.

The voltage of LiPo cells in series are summed in order to determine the overall voltage of the battery pack. For example, a 3S LiPo battery will be capable of supplying a maximum voltage of 12.6 volts and have a nominal voltage of 11.1 volts.

Safe Discharging

LiPo batteries must never be discharged below the critical voltage of 3.0 volts per cell in order to avoid permanent damage to the battery. Therefore, it is prudent to land with no less than 3.25 volts per cell (providing a 20% margin of safety). If using a Return to Home (RTH) failsafe feature, it should be triggered at approximately 3.45 volts per cell, depending on the distance between the home position and the operating area.

Table 1-3 shows the fully charged, nominal, safe discharge, and failsafe voltage levels for various LiPo batteries with cells in series.

Table 1-3. LiPo Battery Voltage Chart

CELLS IN SERIES	FULLY CHARGED VOLTAGE	NOMINAL VOLTAGE	SAFE DISCHARGE VOLTAGE	RTH FAILSAFE VOLTAGE*
1	4.2	3.7	3.25	3.4
2	8.4	7.4	6.5	6.8
3	12.6	11.1	9.75	10.2
4	16.8	14.8	13	13.6
5	21	18.5	16.25	17
6	25.2	22.2	19.5	20.4
7	29.4	25.9	22.75	23.8
8	33.6	29.6	26	27.2

*These voltages are recommendations and may not be suitable for all situations. RTH failsafe voltage should be raised when operating at great distance or in high wind conditions.

Charging

LiPo batteries require a balancing charger to keep the voltage of each of the cells the same while charging. If the voltage of the cells becomes too far out of balance, then the battery pack may become unusable. LiPo battery chargers will have two connection leads: one for the power connector and one for a balance connector.

The power lead is usually connected to the charger with removable banana plugs, which allows batteries with different power connector types to be charged by different charging leads. Another option may be a "charging octopus," which provides multiple power connector types on a single lead. In any case, it is essential to connect the charging lead to the charger before connecting it to the battery in order to avoid short-circuiting the battery by inadvertently contacting the banana plugs.

The balance lead of the charger is connected to the balance lead of the battery and allows the charger to interface with each cell of the battery for balancing. The charger's balancing lead will either include or facilitate the use of a balancing board, which has connector ports for battery balance leads of multiple cell counts mounted to it (Figure 1-32).

When charging, the user will normally need to program the charger for the series cell count and charging current of the specific battery. Some chargers will allow for battery charging profiles to be saved, which makes charging of multiple types of batteries simpler. Other more advanced features to consider include protections against improper connection and the display of charging data such as mAh input, which would allow the operator to understand to what degree the battery had been discharged during the previous flight.

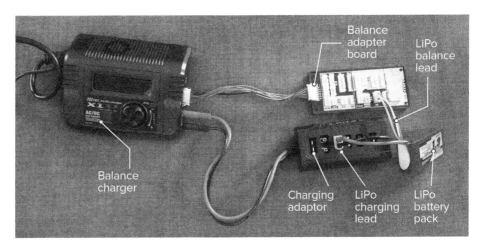

Figure 1-32. LiPo charger components.

Safety Concerns

Damaged LiPo batteries have the potential to explode if damaged or mishandled. For this reason, it is important to follow these safety precautions:

1. Batteries should be charged in a fire-retardant container such as a battery charging bag, which are available from hobby shops.

2. Batteries should never be left unattended while charging.

3. Keep a fire extinguisher and heat-resistant gloves near the battery charging station.

4. In the event of a LiPo fire, it is usually best to allow the battery itself to burn out while controlling the spread of the fire with a fire extinguisher and avoiding exposure to fumes.

5. In the event that a battery becomes severely damaged, keep it submerged in a bath of salt water in a non-metallic container placed in a safe, outdoor area until it is fully discharged and can be disposed of properly based on local regulations. It will usually take 2–3 weeks for a battery to fully discharge in a salt bath.

6. Batteries should be stored and transported in a fireproof container. Military surplus ammo cans can be ideal for this purpose.

7. Batteries that have been crashed, dropped, or similarly abused should be considered suspect and should be retired from regular use. At best, these batteries may still be used for bench testing but only after a thorough inspection.

Storage

If batteries are not used for an extended period of time (longer than two weeks as a rule of thumb), balancing their cells at the nominal voltage will increase the lifespan of the battery. Most chargers will have a storage balancing feature, which will reduce the volatility of the battery as well as the likelihood that the voltage of the cells will drop below critical voltage. Storage balancing batteries can be very important in areas where flying is not possible year round. Similarly, extreme cold can adversely affect a battery's charge level and lifespan. Batteries should be stored in a climate-controlled area, and when it is necessary to operate in extreme cold, batteries should be kept as close as possible to room temperature until ready for use (as well as after use).

Flight Controller

Flight controllers are the brains of autonomous vehicles and are sometimes referred to as autopilots, but this is a misnomer. In its broadest and most basic definition, a flight controller is a computer processor on board an aircraft that converts inputs, including user commands and sensor data, into outputs to the maneuvering controls for the purpose of maintaining stable flight. While a flight controller is required for autonomous flight, not all flight controllers are inherently capable of acting as an autopilot in the traditional sense.

For example, all RC multicopters require at least a very basic flight controller to convert inputs from the user (via the RC receiver) into appropriate RPM commands, which are sent to the individual motors in order to produce the desired maneuvers. This is mainly due to two characteristics of multicopters: (1) maneuvering inputs about a single axis will require changes in response from each motor in a multicopter arrangement, and (2) multicopter airframes are inherently unstable, and so in order to achieve stability, they require intervention from a flight controller to provide complex control responses faster than a human could provide. Therefore, in a multicopter configuration, a flight controller will receive maneuvering inputs for each control axis through individual ports and output commands through individual motor ports *(Figure 1-33)*.

However, unlike multicopters, in RC airplanes: (1) control commands about a single axis generally translate directly to the movement of a single servo or to pairs of servos working in tandem, and (2) when built correctly, most airplanes are much more aerodynamically stable than multicopters. Therefore, RC airplanes have existed for decades without flight controllers; however, flight controllers can be incorporated in order to achieve greater navigational stability and accuracy *(Figure 1-34)*.

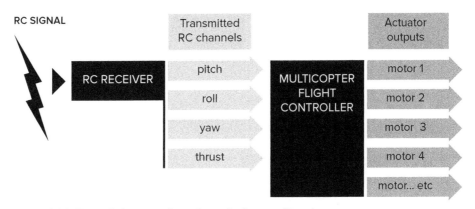

Figure 1-33. Basic flight controller schematic for a multicopter.

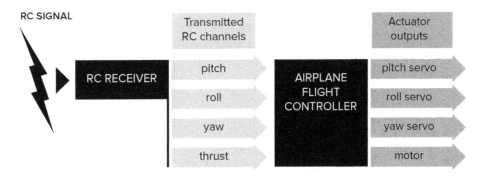

Figure 1-34. Basic flight controller schematic for an airplane.

More advanced flight controller systems usually include sensors such as an inertial measurement unit (IMU), GPS receiver, and compass in order to stabilize the aircraft and maintain position. Some systems incorporating these sensors are capable of various flight control modes or even returning the aircraft to its takeoff location as a failsafe. However, this does not necessarily mean that the system is capable of executing a flight plan automatically (the main benchmark of an autonomous vehicle). This ability necessitates onboard memory, allowing the flight plan to be stored on the aircraft, and some means of interfacing with flight planning software, preferably a telemetry link *(Figure 1-35)*.

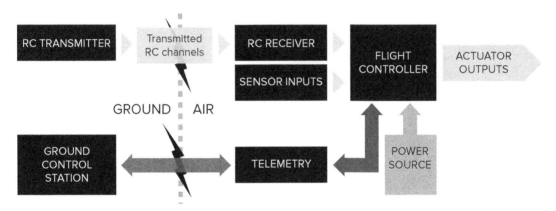

Figure 1-35. Basic Schematic of Unmanned Aircraft Components.

Flight Controller Sensors

/ GPS/COMPASS UNIT

The **Global Positioning System (GPS)** has become pervasive in modern society, as it is now incorporated into most smartphones and tablets. The system relies on a group of satellites in geosynchronous orbit, meaning each satellite orbits at the same rotational speed of the Earth and thus maintains its position over the Earth's surface. Each satellite transmits a radio signal with a very accurate time stamp, which is received by a GPS receiver on the ground. The receiver then uses this information to calculate its distance from multiple satellites and triangulate its own position on the surface of the Earth. Signals from four satellites are required to determine a three-dimensional location, usually expressed in latitude, longitude, and altitude. It is not unrealistic to receive signals from 10 to 15 satellites, although it may take some time after power up to acquire satellites. GPS systems used in civilian UAs generally provide location accuracy within three meters or less.

It is important to remember that the GPS receiver does not provide any data regarding the direction that the aircraft is pointing, but it can be used to determine direction of travel and ground speed when the aircraft is in motion. The electronic compass unit or magnetometer is a magnetic device that determines the heading to magnetic north. This heading can then be compared to the heading of the aircraft for the purpose of navigation. Some flight controllers will apply local magnetic declination (the difference between true north and magnetic north) based on GPS position so that the aircraft can operate based on true heading. The compass unit is heavily affected by local magnetic fields, which can vary greatly between flying sites; therefore, regular compass calibrations are a prudent part of preflight (discussed further in Chapter 2).

Figure 1-36. GPS/compass mast.

Many systems incorporate the GPS receiver and compass into a single unit. These devices are very susceptible to interference from high voltage sources such as batteries, power distribution boards (PDBs), and electronic speed controllers (ESCs). Therefore, it is best to physically separate the GPS/compass unit from these components. This can be accomplished by mounting the GPS/compass unit atop a mast on multicopters (*Figure 1-36*) or on the tail booms of airplanes and helicopters. This accomplishes another important requirement for proper GPS receiver function by giving it a clear view of the sky, thus improving signal reception from the satellites. If this is not possible, copper or copper mesh tape can help to isolate the unit from some interference. Carbon fiber can also adversely affect these components when in close proximity. The GPS receiver can be affected by interference from other transmitters on the aircraft, such as a 1.3 MHz video signal. This can be addressed through the use of filters and/or a power switch for the video transmitter (discussed later in this chapter under Imaging Sensor Payloads). Finally, it is very important that the compass unit is installed pointing in the correct direction relative to the front of the aircraft and consistent with the settings of the flight controller.

/ INERTIAL MEASUREMENT UNIT (IMU)

The **inertial measurement unit** (IMU) or accelerometer is used to measure the aircraft's orientation with regard to the three axes as well as the aircraft's translational and rotational movement about these axes (*Figure 1-37*). This data is used by the flight controller to stabilize the aircraft and maintain coordination during maneuvers. The IMU information can also be directly conveyed to the user through telemetry and displayed as the artificial horizon or attitude indicator on the ground control station and in the video signal with on-screen display (OSD) overlay. Whether the IMU is incorporated internally into the flight controller or is a separate external unit, it is important that it is securely mounted in the proper orientation relative to the front of

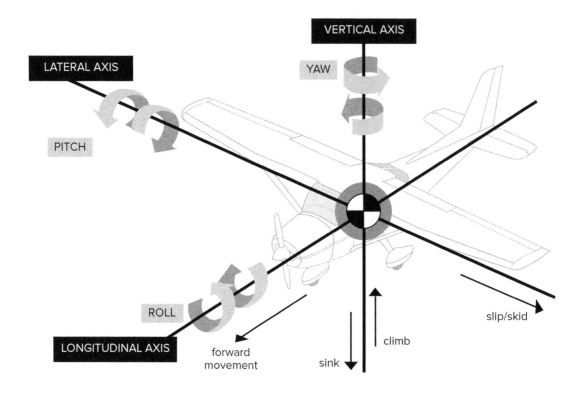

Figure 1-37. Aircraft translation and rotation measured by the IMU.

the aircraft, while also being isolated against vibrations. IMUs can be adversely affected by crashes or rough landings, and thus regular checks of IMU fidelity, and calibrations if necessary, are a prudent part of preflight (covered in detail in Chapter 6).

/ POWER MANAGEMENT UNIT (PMU)

The power management unit (PMU) performs a basic function as part of the electrical system by providing regulated power to the flight controller. Some PMUs can also be considered sensors in that they provide battery voltage and current draw information to the flight controller. This information can in turn be transmitted to the ground control station via the telemetry link to be monitored by the operator as well as used by the flight controller to trigger failsafe contingencies at a predetermined low battery voltage. *It is important to understand the voltage limits of the PMU, which is usually expressed in terms of LiPo battery cell count, before connecting to power.*

/ PITOT TUBE/AIRSPEED SENSOR

For multicopters and helicopters, the GPS can be used to determine the aircraft speed over the ground (ground speed). However, flight controllers on airplanes are heavily dependent on accurate measurements of the aircraft's speed through the air (airspeed) to avoid stall, especially during landing. This is accomplished through the use of a pitot tube, which uses differences in total and static air pressure to determine airspeed *(Figure 1-38)*. A pitot tube should be mounted so that the tube is pointed directly forward relative to the front of the aircraft, commonly mounted to the leading edge of the wing or the side of the fuselage but removed from the turbulent air created behind propellers *(Figure 1-39)*. The pitot tube can be susceptible to blockage from debris and should be checked prior to each flight. Airspeed sensors can also be drastically affected by temperature variations and usually require frequent calibration to maintain accuracy.

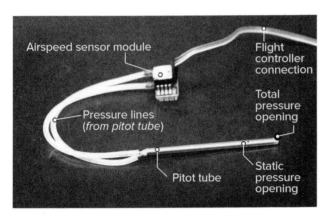

Figure 1-38. Airspeed sensor and pitot tube.

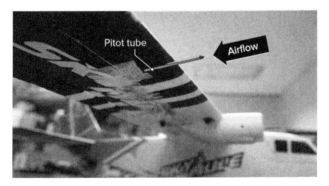

Figure 1-39. Pitot tube mounting.

/ RANGE SENSOR

A range sensor, such as a sonar module, can be used on rotor-wing aircraft to accurately determine the aircraft's height above the ground or a structure. This information may also be used to control the descent rate during landing or kill the engines when on the ground. In a fixed-wing aircraft, data from such a sensor can be used during landing to adjust the glideslope as well as to flare and kill the motors at a safe height above the ground. These systems generally have a range of approximately 7 to 10 meters above the ground and can be significantly affected by the type of surface being detected.

/ OPTICAL FLOW SENSOR

An optical flow sensor is essentially a low-resolution camera and processor that can be used by a flight controller on a rotor-wing aircraft to maintain a constant hover position. In some cases, this positioning method can be more effective than GPS (for holding position, not for navigation) and may be used by some flight controllers in the event that GPS is lost. However, the effectiveness of these optical systems is very dependent on lighting as well as the type of surface being detected, and they are generally only effective at low altitude.

Telemetry Unit

A **telemetry unit** is a radio module that transmits and receives data, such as aircraft telemetry and operator commands, between the aircraft and the ground. One such transceiver is installed on the aircraft, and another is part of the ground control station. The airborne component of the telemetry system is usually proprietarily linked to the flight controller facilities by two-way wireless data transmission between the aircraft and the ground station.

When functioning properly, these units do not require much interface from the user. However, some telemetry units will provide frequency, amplitude, and data transmission rate settings, which can be adjusted by the operator. The air and ground units may also need to be paired or otherwise configured for their function. Finally, some ground units will require external power whereas others are powered through their interface with the ground control device.

Maneuvering Controls

/ SERVOS

Servos are used primarily to physically move control surfaces on airplanes and articulate swash plates on helicopters. They can also be adapted to move other aircraft components, such as landing gear, camera mounts, and bay doors.

Theory of Operation

A servo will receive power (usually 5 V) and PWM information through a standard three-wire RC connection, causing a tiny gear protruding from the servo casing to reposition itself based on the current PWM value received. The center of this gear is usually threaded, allowing a small arm called a servo horn to be secured to the gear. The servo horn contains a row of small holes, which can be attached to one end of a control rod (*Figure 1-40*).

The other end of this rod is attached to another small arm that resembles the servo horn and is secured to a control surface (*Figure 1-41*). At least one end of the rod should be connected with an adjustable linkage allowing the control surface to be mechanically centered. In this configuration, the flight controller sends a PWM value to the servo causing it to rotate the servo horn to the corresponding position, which in turn translates the control rod longitudinally and rotates the control surface about its hinged axis.

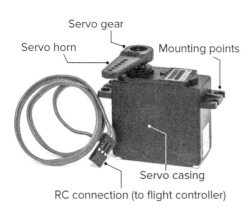

Servo gear

Servo horn

Mounting points

Servo casing

RC connection (to flight controller)

Figure 1-40. An RC servo.
(*iStock.com/birdeyeistock*)

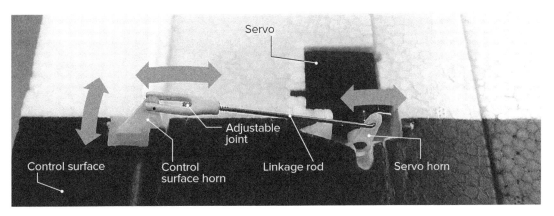

Figure 1-41. Servo linkages.

Types of Servos

Servos are rated by size and the amount of force they are capable of applying. Most off-the-shelf RC airplanes and helicopters have, at the very least, mounting positions installed or cut for specific sizes of servos as well as recommended specifications for the servos to be used.

Some servos have metal gears rather than plastic ones. These are more resistant to damage, binding, and wear but are slightly heavier and more expensive.

Servos are available in digital and analog varieties. Digital servos provide more precise control and a smaller dead band around their neutral rotation position. This provides improved control of the precise movements that are required of helicopter swashplates. Digital servos are generally expensive and may not be supported by all RC transceiver systems.

Most servos have rotation limits, but so-called 360-degree servos allow for completer rotation. These servos work especially well for the panning of camera mounts.

Servo Configurations

Each individual control surface generally requires a separate servo; however, there are some exceptions such as single-servo aileron and flap setups as well as V-tails. Figure 1-42 reviews the servo configurations as previously described in detail in the Airplane Theory section earlier in this chapter.

Proper Set Up and Operation

The RC connector should be connected to the appropriate output port on the flight controller. After powering, observe the deflection of servos based on the appropriate RC stick input, and reverse the servo channel through the flight controller if necessary. If the corresponding RC stick is then returned to its center position, the servo will go to its neutral position. With the neutral position found, attach the servo horn

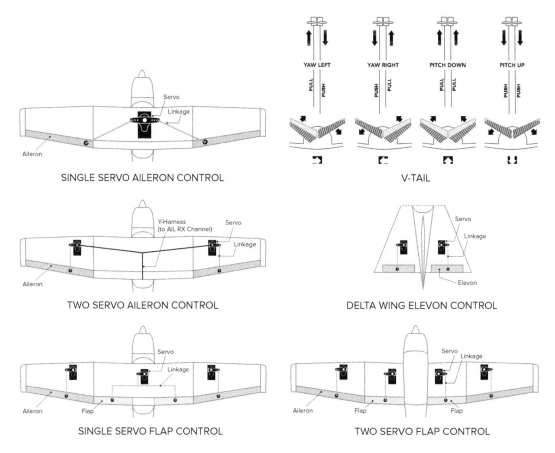

Figure 1-42. Servo configurations.

so that it is at the center of its intended travel arc once installed *(Figure 1-43)*. For example, on an airplane with the aileron servos mounted to the underside of the wing, the servo horn should point generally straight down when the servo is in its neutral position. This will give the servo its maximum range of motion both forward and backward.

Be sure to power off the system before installing the servo horn screw, as special care should be taken to avoid stripping the internal servo gears, especially when power is applied. In short, do not disturb the servos when the system is on, and move the servos only gently when the system is off.

Next, the servo can be secured in its mounting position with screws having either threadlocker or lock washers. The control rod may also be installed in the servo horn with the other end left disconnected from the control surface horn. Connecting the control rod further from the center of the servo horn will result in greater range of motion of the control rod but more torque on the servo. With the system powered

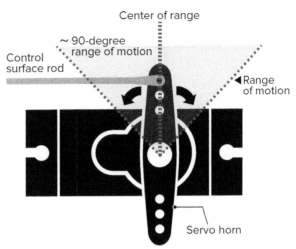

Figure 1-43. Servo neutral position and range of motion.

on again and the servo horn at its neutral position, note the location of the control surface horn attachment along the length of the control rod when the trailing edge of the control surface is lined up with the trailing edge of the wing or tail. This is considered the neutral position of the control surface. Power the system off while you make these adjustments to the control rod. Sliding servo horn attachments with set screws make these adjustments easier, but they tend to be less secure than the clevis or ball-type attachments *(Figure 1-44)*.

Check that both ends of the control rod are secure and do not slip before powering the system on again to check the control surface movement. The servos may make some noise, but a high-pitched squealing sound indicates binding or stripping of the gears. Also, the control rod should not bend when the control surface is deflected; this would indicate that the horn attachments are not rotating properly or that the servo is trying to force the control surface beyond its physical limits. In this case, the range of motion of the servo should be changed, either mechanically using another hole on the servo horn or electronically by setting limits in the flight controller. Repeat this process as necessary for the rest of the servos on the aircraft.

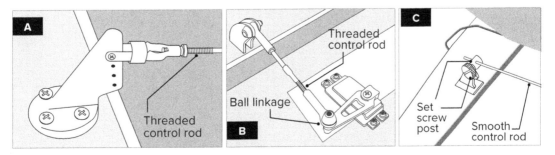

Figure 1-44. Types of control rod linkages: (A) threaded clevis, (B) threaded ball joint, and (C) set screw.

/ ELECTRONIC SPEED CONTROLLERS (ESCs)

Electronic speed controllers (ESCs) are used to convert the direct current (DC) provided by the flight battery into the alternating current (AC) required to operate brushless motors (discussed later in this chapter). ESCs usually consist of a rectangular circuit board wrapped in heat shrink or casing with sets of wires extending from either end (*Figure 1-45*). The inboard set of wires provide the inputs to the ESC and consist of a standard three-wire servo connector for control inputs and two usually large-gauge wires for power input. The power wires are shielded with red insulation for the positive lead and black insulation for the negative (or ground) lead.

On the opposite end of the ESC, the outboard or output wires are used to connect the three leads on the brushless motors. These wires may be labeled A, B, and C and/or have different-colored insulation, but they are interchangeable. In fact, the rotation direction of a motor may be reversed by swapping any two of the connections, using the colors or labels for reference. These three leads are used to alternate the magnetic polarity of pole sets within the brushless motor, causing the motor to spin. The rate at which this polarity alternates is controlled by the ESC, based on commands from the flight controller, thus determining the RPM of the motor.

Selecting ESCs

ESCs are rated by the maximum amperage that these devices can handle. When selecting ESCs, it is important to look for an amperage rating which is at least 20% greater than the maximum current draw of the motor during normal operations. This provides for a margin of error in order to deal with current spikes caused by windy or turbulent conditions. ESCs are also designed for a certain voltage range, usually

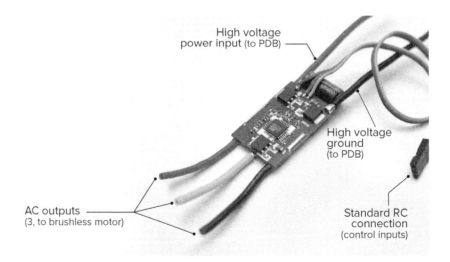

High voltage power input (to PDB)

High voltage ground (to PDB)

AC outputs (3, to brushless motor)

Standard RC connection (control inputs)

Figure 1-45. An electronic speed controller (ESC). *(ESC for hobby use rated at 35 Amps of power; Avsar Aras; https://commons.wikimedia.org/wiki/File:ESC_35A.jpg; CC BY-SA 3.0)*

expressed in terms of LiPo cell count, and therefore it is important to verify that an ESC can handle the voltage from the intended battery. Other ESC features such as internal BECs and OPTO isolations (see "ESCs on Multicopters" section later in this chapter) are important to consider based on airframe type.

ESCs on Airplanes

As described previously and shown in Figure 1-29, battery eliminator circuits (BECs) incorporated into ESCs are the primary source of power for the RC receiver, flight controller, and servos on the aircraft. In this case, the power leads of the ESC are connected directly to the PMU. The ESC servo lead connects to the flight controller with the red wire, carrying lower voltage to power all servos that are connected to the flight controller through a common power rail. Remember, BECs are designed to accommodate only particular cell count LiPo batteries and a certain number of servos within a system, so it is important to consider this before purchasing an ESC with an internal BEC.

ESCs on Multicopters

On a multicopter airframe, the power leads from the ESCs are connected to the appropriate terminals of the PDB, which is usually centrally located. The servo leads are connected to the appropriate numbered output port for that motor position on the flight controller. It is generally advisable to use identical ESCs on each motor. Even if a multicopter incorporates servos, such as in a tricopter configuration or on an articulating camera mount, it is not necessary to have multiple BEC inputs connected to the power rail of the flight controller. Therefore, OPTO ESCs—which do not incorporate internal BECs and are isolated against electrical failures—in addition to a single external BEC, are best for multicopters.

Programming and Calibrating ESCs

Some ESCs can be programmed with various features using either an external programming card or a connection to computer software. This includes features such as motor braking (used to prevent the propeller from idly spinning or "windmilling" when the motor is off during landing, thus preventing damage to the propeller when the aircraft contacts the ground), start and stop mode, and cut off voltage.

Many ESCs also require calibration, which consists of setting the minimum and maximum throttle settings for the RC system receiver. This is usually accomplished by connecting an ESC directly to the RC receiver throttle channel (usually channel 3) while power is applied, entering the ESC calibration mode, and running the throttle stick to its maximum and minimum positions.

It is especially important that ESCs on multicopters be calibrated—and calibrated identically—so that in a steady, level hover, all motors are spinning at the same RPM for a given throttle setting. Some flight controllers provide special modes that allow all ESCs to be calibrated at once, but the same action can be accomplished with a multiple output harness or adapter. Consult the ESC user documentation to determine the correct calibration procedure.

ESC Sounds

Many ESCs are capable of emitting sounds or musical tones to indicate modes or to confirm programming. Tones are usually used to indicate when an ESC has been placed in calibration mode and again when calibration is complete. An ESC's user documentation often tries to describe these tones, but it is a good idea to also consult demonstration videos for the calibration procedure if they are available. ESCs will also emit a tone after power on to indicate that the ESCs are online, and another tone to indicate that they are receiving a low throttle PWM control signal. A safety feature of most flight controllers specifies that the system will not provide a PWM signal to ESCs until the system is armed by the user. This can result in the ESCs emitting regular, annoying beeps indicating the lack of input. If this becomes too obnoxious while working on the aircraft, it can often be remedied by arming and disarming the aircraft while observing any appropriate safety precautions if the propellers are mounted to the motors.

Propulsion Systems

/ BRUSHLESS MOTORS

Electric **brushless motors** are now the standard for RC aircraft propulsion. The term "brushless" refers to the fact that no electrical contact occurs between the stationary portion of the motor and the rotating portion, or bell. Therefore, there is no "spark" between these two portions as might be observed in a brushed motor.

The most common type of brushless motor used in RC aircraft today is referred to as an outrunner, in which the rotating motor bell is on the outside of the motor (*Figure 1-46*). These brushless motors operate by altering the magnetic field through coils of wire that are wrapped around a spoked stator within the motor housing. These

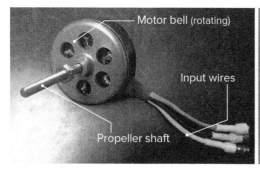
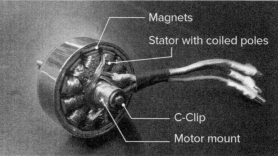

Figure 1-46. Components of an outrunner brushless motor.

coils form magnetic poles arranged in a circular pattern and are usually insulated from each other with a special coating. Each of these coils is connected to one of the three brushless motor input wires that carry signals from the ESC. The ESC controls the current through each of these wires separately, and by pushing, reversing, or halting the currents, the polarity of each of the coils will be positive, negative, or neutral at a given instant. These polarities will interact with a series of magnets or poles arranged by alternating polarity around the inner circumference of the motor bell. The currents coming from the ESCs will in effect "rotate" polarities of the stator coils at a speed determined by the throttle input coming from the pilot via the flight controller, which will in turn rotate the motor bell to which the propeller is mounted.

Because brushless motors really have only one moving part, and very little contact occurs between parts, brushless motors tend to be less likely to wear out than their predecessors. The most likely point of failure is usually the bearing, which is the only interface between moving parts and is held in place with a small C-clip on the underside of the motor.

Brushless Motor Designations

Unfortunately, no standard currently exists among brushless motor manufacturers for assigning numerical designations to motors. Therefore, different companies will number their motor models using very different conventions. The most common information found in motor numbers denotes the physical size of the motor. Usually, a four-digit number sequence will contain the circumference of the motor (first two digits) and the length or height of the motor (last two digits), both given in millimeters. However, some motor manufacturers may include the diameter of the stator rather than the outer diameter of the motor. Motor designations may also include the number of poles or the number of wire windings within each stator coil. Refer to the manufacturer's documentation or specifications to determine what motor designation numbering system is used for a specific motor.

Important Motor Information

The most important motor information to consider is usually not contained within manufacturer designations but is commonly advertised. The first important consideration describes the maximum speed at which a motor will spin, which is a function of the voltage of the battery. Therefore, brushless motors will be assigned a kilovolt (kV) term, which is a measure of RPM x 1000 per volt. In general, higher kV motors will spin a propeller faster but rarely provide much torque. Therefore, they are not capable of spinning larger, heavier propellers and are better suited for smaller aircraft. Lower kV motors, on the other hand, are capable of spinning larger propellers but at lower speeds, and tend to be more efficient. These low-kV motors are sometimes referred to as "pancake" motors because they usually have a larger diameter but a smaller height or length. The other important consideration is the maximum current draw of a motor, as this may be used to properly select ESCs.

/ PROPELLERS

Propellers are generally rated in terms of their diameter, which is relatively easy to understand, and blade pitch, a more abstract concept. The pitch of the blades is normally measured in inches and represents the distance the propeller would advance if it were to complete one full revolution, cutting through the air unaffected by slip or drag. Propellers are usually marked as *propeller diameter* x *blade pitch*, so a 10 x 5 propeller will have a 10-inch diameter and a 5-inch blade pitch.

RC propellers usually have between two and four blades. A propeller with more blades will be capable of generating more thrust but is less efficient, due to both the added mass of more blades and the increased turbulence each blade must pass through (caused by the more closely spaced preceding blade). Propellers with more than two blades are intended mainly for aesthetic appearance on scale model aircraft.

Materials

RC scale propellers are commonly available in wood, plastic, and carbon fiber.

The first RC propellers were manufactured from wood and tended to be rather heavy and to splinter when broken. Also, because of the heterogeneous nature of wood, these propellers often required balancing to avoid producing damaging vibrations. Wood propellers are still available and used in the RC hobby, particularly for aesthetics in scale models.

Plastic or plastic composite propellers have become more available and popular in recent years, as they are generally affordable and can be incredibly resilient with composite fillers. If they do fail, plastic propellers tend to crack rather than splinter, making them safer. However, they are not always manufactured with the tightest tolerances and will sometimes require balancing.

Carbon fiber propellers are usually very light and well-manufactured. The disadvantages of this type of propeller include the fact that carbon fiber can splinter dangerously and can interfere with radio signals. Carbon fiber propellers are also relatively expensive.

Balancing of Propellers

Regardless of the type of material used, it is possible for one propeller blade to be heavier than the other(s). This may be the result of a manufacturing error or of uneven material distribution. In any case, it can be beneficial, especially if attempting to reduce vibrations, to check the balance of propellers before installation by using a propeller balancing tool *(Figure 1-47)*. These balancers generally hold a propeller on a near frictionless pivot. If the propeller rotates, then the blades are out of balance. In order to balance a propeller, some pilots will lightly sand the underside of the tip of the heavier blade. However, this may affect the aerodynamics of the blade, which obviously should be avoided. Along these lines, it is a good idea to lightly sand or

Figure 1-47.
A magnetic propeller balancing tool.

cut away the mold seams of plastic propellers, as the seams can form a sharp edge along the leading and trailing edges. Arguably the best method for balancing a propeller is to add a light coat of sandable paint to the tips of the propellers prior to balancing. Then if necessary, a small amount may be sanded from the heavier blade. Using a brightly colored paint will also increase the visibility of a spinning propeller for safety during flight operations.

Imaging Sensor Payloads

The most common unmanned payloads involve carrying a camera or other form of imaging sensor. There are three basic configurations of these payloads: surveying, FPV reconnaissance, and **FPV** pilot camera. The term FPV stands for **first-person view**—RC shorthand for the ability of personnel on the ground to monitor a live video feed from the viewpoint of the aircraft in flight.

/ SURVEYING

The surveying payload configuration uses a camera or sensor, generally pointed downward, to take a series of still images of the Earth's surface while the aircraft flies back and forth over an area defined in the mission plan. After the flight, the GPS, attitude, and altitude information found in the flight controller mission logs may be used to stitch these images together into a large, high-resolution image or map of the area surveyed. This data is valuable in agriculture, mining, and mapping, in many cases replacing satellite imagery, which tends to be lower resolution, affected by cloud cover, and less timely.

Components

Camera/Imaging Sensor—The type of camera or sensor used will depend on the data being collected. Factors to consider include resolution of the sensor, focusing capability, and triggering rate. Because images will be recorded during the flight rather than transmitted, the camera must have sufficient internal memory, usually in the form of a removable SD card.

Camera Mount—The camera or sensor will require a fixed or articulating mount to attach it to the aircraft airframe. A **fixed mount** is the simplest form of mounting device and keeps the camera in a fixed position, oriented downward relative to the aircraft. An **articulating mount** attaches the camera or sensor to a movable tray and uses a pair of servos or other actuators to keep the camera pointed downward relative to the Earth (referred to as the Nadir position), which may improve the quality of certain data sets. An articulating mount may also be used to orient the camera in directions other than downward for different purposes, such as for generating 3D imagery of a structure or for stowing the camera to prevent it from being damaged during takeoff and landing. Some flight controllers provide means for controlling the servos of an articulating mount through their output ports. A gimbal (discussed in the FPV reconnaissance section below), capable of providing the most stable camera pointing, may substitute for an articulating mount, but not vice versa. In many surveying cases, operators will find that gimbals provide the best image quality.

Photo Triggering Mechanism—This payload configuration also requires a method for allowing the flight controller to trigger the camera to take a picture. This allows the photo survey tool, which is commonly incorporated into mission planning software, to create survey missions and trigger the camera at regular intervals as required by the processing software. This can be accomplished by physically actuating the camera trigger button. A more elegant solution is to use an infrared (IR) triggering mechanism mounted over the IR sensor of the camera. These mechanisms interface with a servo port of the flight controller and emit an IR flash to signal the camera to take a picture. Finally, some cameras will allow for external triggering via a USB cable. Many modern gimbals and mounts that are designed to support specific camera models include integrated methods of triggering still images or video. In any case, these are important considerations when selecting a camera and/or mount.

/ FPV RECONNAISSANCE

The FPV reconnaissance payload configuration is very similar to what the military has utilized in employing unmanned vehicles, using a camera or imaging sensor to search for or look at an object on the ground. This type of payload can be useful in professional video production, structural inspection, and search and rescue applications.

Components

Camera—Once again, the type of camera selected will depend on the specific application. Professional video operations will usually favor cameras capable of HD recording and the option for interchangeable lenses. Inspection and search operations, on the other hand, may benefit from sensors or combinations of sensors that cover multiple spectrums, such as thermal and IR. In many cases, but especially in professional video operations, the low-resolution FPV signal is used to compose shots through the motion of the aircraft and the gimbal. Meanwhile, this video is simultaneously recorded in high resolution on the camera's internal memory. Therefore, selecting a camera that is capable of both video output and internal recording can be essential.

Camera Gimbal—The FPV reconnaissance configuration requires the ability to orient the camera at an object on the ground regardless of the attitude of the aircraft. This requires the use of a stabilized mount, commonly referred to as a **gimbal**, which allows the user to control the orientation while the aircraft maneuvers (*Figure 1-48*). To accomplish this, most gimbals use brushless motors, controlled by a **gimbal**

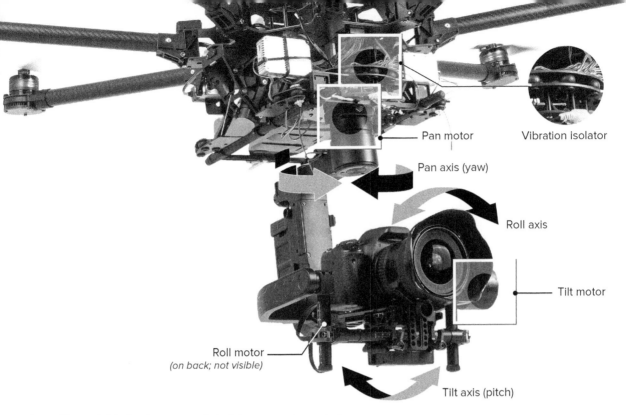

Figure 1-48. 3-axis camera gimbal. (*iStock.com/seregalsv*)

control unit (GCU), to orient the camera. The GCU functions similarly to a flight controller, with an internal accelerometer or IMU providing information about the aircraft's attitude, but allows separate processing power to be devoted to stabilizing the gimbal at a high frequency. GCUs also operate on proportional-integral-derivative (PID) loops (discussed in Chapter 5), which in most cases may be tuned using external companion software producing better stabilization response about the roll, tilt (pitch), and pan (yaw) axes of the camera. Before tuning, however, the camera should be properly balanced on the gimbal, meaning that when the gimbal is powered off and the motors may spin freely, the camera will generally maintain any orientation that it is placed in. Balancing may require adjusting the position of the camera on the gimbal's mounting tray or adding small amounts of weight to the structure of the gimbal.

Video Transmitter—The FPV reconnaissance payload configuration also requires a video transmitter on board the aircraft as well as a video receiver and monitor as part of the on-ground payload support equipment. These systems are generally available in 2.4 GHz, which is the most common, and a lower frequency of 1.3 GHz, which may provide longer range but requires a larger antenna and may interfere with GPS signals. The implementation of these systems is described in detail in the following sections.

/ FPV PILOT CAMERA

The FPV pilot camera configuration provides a live video feed from the perspective of the aircraft, as if a tiny pilot were sitting in it. This allows pilots flying in an RC mode better control over aircraft maneuvers. While common in hobby aircraft like racing multicopters, this configuration is rarely used on its own in commercial aircraft but rather to improve performance and safety of aircraft equipped with the surveying or FPV reconnaissance configurations. For example, an FPV pilot camera on a structural inspection aircraft would improve the pilot's ability to avoid obstacles while travelling to the observation position required by the mission. In fact, some gimbals and articulating mounts may allow a camera to be stowed forward in a pilot camera position, providing the same perspective.

Components

Camera—This configuration frequently uses so-called **board cameras**, essentially tiny spy cameras that are usually mounted on small circuit boards. Having no internal recording capability, these cameras are typically light and compact, allowing them to be easily mounted onto the aircraft. While generally inexpensive, the quality of these cameras is usually directly proportional to their price.

Video Transmitter—Some board cameras are now available with integrated video transmitters and permanently mounted antennas. This may greatly simplify the integration of FPV pilot cams. However, separate video transmitters should be considered in cases where collocating the camera and the video transmitter would be prevented by the structure of the aircraft or due to signal interference. External video transmitters can also provide more options as far as channels and output power.

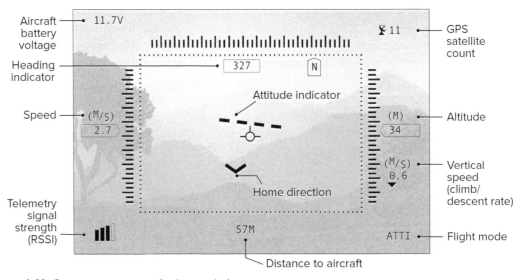

Figure 1-49. Common on-screen display symbology.

On-Screen Display (OSD)—This payload configuration is greatly improved by the use of an **on-screen display** (**OSD**) module, a component installed on board the aircraft that visually overlays data taken from the flight controller telemetry onto the video feed (*Figure 1-49*). When viewed on the monitor, this data appears similar to a heads-up display (HUD) system used on military aircraft, providing the pilot with greater awareness of the aircraft's status.

/ BASIC AIRBORNE FPV IMPLEMENTATION

The illustration in Figure 1-50 shows the implementation of an airborne FPV system.

Many GCUs, OSDs, and video transmitters will come with premade connector cables for video and power, but these leads may require modification (soldering on longer wires, different connectors, etc.) to interface properly with your system. On these components, look for connector pins labeled "video in" and "video out" (yellow wires), "power in" (red wire), and "power out" (red wire; on some video TXs to supply power to a board camera). Remember that connections between two components require at least one ground (black wire) (*Figure 1-51*).

Note that GCUs and OSDs will generally accept a range of voltages, but almost all video transmitters require a 12-volt power supply, which will necessitate a BEC if using a battery with more than three cells. Also, RC channels controlling the gimbal may be taken directly from the RC receiver or—if using a Futaba S.Bus protocol, Spektrum Satellite, or other form of PPM encoding—from the flight controller camera mount control outputs, with the applicable gains set to zero so that stabilization is applied only by the GCU. In this case, the OSD module is optional but recommended. Be sure to select an OSD that is compatible with the flight controller and its telemetry protocol.

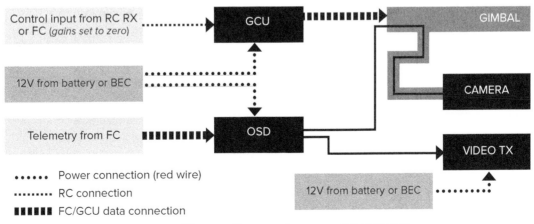

All connections require a ground (not shown)

Figure 1-50. Basic FPV system.

Battery ground (black)
Battery power (red)
Antenna
GND
BATT
AUDR
AUDL
VID In
GND
+5v Out
Audio (not necessary)
Video Signal (Yellow, to camera)
Video Ground (Black, to camera)
Camera Power (Red, optional)

Figure 1-51. Example video transmitter.

/ ADVANCED AIRBORNE FPV IMPLEMENTATION

If using a larger digital single-lens reflex (DSLR) or similar camera on a gimbal to produce cinematic professional video, a two-operator system is recommended. This allows a pilot to concentrate on flying the aircraft along the intended path while the payload operator is free to control the gimbal and frame the shot properly. This does require two RC transmitters on the ground and two RC receivers on the aircraft. Many new operators will initially insist that they can both fly the aircraft and operate the gimbal, but monitoring both the position of the aircraft and the orientation of the shot has consistently proven to impose excessive workload on a single operator.

You may also consider implementing a system with both a pilot camera and a gimbal, necessitating two video transmitters on the aircraft and two monitors on the ground. Such a system, illustrated in Figure 1-52, incorporates several new components, which are described below.

In this system, the gimbal and camera are connected similarly to Figure 1-50, but receive control inputs from a dedicated payload operator via a second RC receiver. The video output signal is then routed from the camera and gimbal to an optional high-definition to standard (HD-to-AV) video converter, which may be required in order to convert a high-definition video signal from the camera into a standard AV signal that can be processed by the video transmitter(s). The video output is then split into two branches, the first going directly to a 5.8 GHz video transmitter and transmitted to the payload operator's video monitor on the ground.

The second branch of the video output is sent to a video switch, a device that interfaces with a standard RC PWM connection (in this case the pilot's RC receiver) in order to select between multiple video signals. When properly configured, the video switch will allow the pilot to use a switch on the RC transmitter to select which signal is sent to the pilot's video monitor—the signal either from the pilot camera or from the camera on the gimbal. The output of the video switch is sent to the OSD and then to the second, 1.3 GHz video transmitter so that the video signal selected by the pilot is overlaid with the OSD data.

Another commonly available video transmission frequency is 1.3 GHz, which can provide a longer range than the 5.8 GHz frequency. In general, lower frequencies provide longer ranges, which may also be achieved through increased transmission power (though the FCC regulates the power of unlicensed transmitters, to under 1 watt in this case). The longer range does, however, come with a price: the 1.3 GHz frequency shares harmonics with the aircraft GPS antenna. This means that the waveform the video transmitter emits will intermittently match that which the GPS antenna is designed to receive, and this can interfere with proper GPS reception. This can be remedied in two ways, best used in conjunction with each other: (1) installing a 2.4 GHz attenuating filter on the antenna of the video transmitter to help reduce some of the harmonics, and (2) installing a separate power switch on the video transmitter to allow it to be powered on separately from the rest of the aircraft. Powering on the aircraft before the 1.3 GHz video transmitter will allow the GPS to establish lock without interference. Once lock is established, powering on the 1.3 GHz video transmitter is less likely to affect GPS signals.

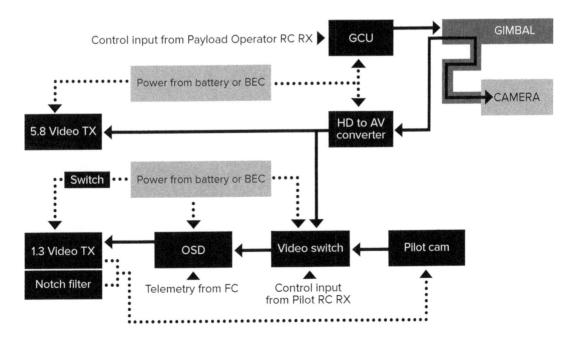

Figure 1-52. Advanced FPV system.

Connecting the pilot camera to the longer-range video transmitter allows for greater safety when it is depended upon to maneuver the aircraft. However, the video switch allows either video source to be transmitted on the longer-range frequency if necessary. Also note that the GCU, HD-to-AV converter, pilot camera, video switch, OSD module, and both video transmitters require the appropriate power supply from the main flight battery, a separate battery, or from a BEC.

/ FPV GROUND SUPPORT EQUIPMENT

FPV requires three basic components as part of the ground station:

- Video receiver
- Monitor
- Power supply

In the past, these components were separate and would need to be modified to interface with each other. Recently, several companies have begun manufacturing monitors with internal rechargeable batteries and 5.8 GHz video receivers. These monitors are now the best solution for the FPV ground station. However, it is important to remember that if using a 1.3 GHz video signal, an external 1.3 GHz video receiver will need to be installed rather than using the internal 5.8 GHz receiver. These monitors may then be mounted to the RC receiver for easy viewing by the pilot (*Figure 1-53*).

Another solution is to use FPV goggles, which generally also incorporate an internal 5.8 GHz video receiver and rechargeable battery but are not adversely affected by bright light as are FPV monitors (*Figure 1-54*). However, these goggles tend to be disorienting to some pilots who may be accustomed to viewing the aircraft directly as is done in normal RC flight. That being said, FPV goggles may be an excellent solution for payload operators who are focusing on framing shots.

Figure 1-53. FPV monitors. *(Left: © leungchopan/Fotolia. Right: iStock.com/aerogondo)*

/ IMPROVING VIDEO SIGNAL

There are several components and strategies to consider when attempting to improve video signals, including cloverleaf antennas, directional antennas, antenna placement, and diversity receivers.

Cloverleaf Antennas

Most video transmitters and receivers will come with familiar "whip" antennas. However, these antennas usually produce blind spots of degraded signals in the direction that the antenna is pointing, and thus their orientation can significantly affect reception. "Cloverleaf" antennas provide a more omnidirectional signal, which may provide a clearer video picture as the aircraft maneuvers and in areas of greater structural interference *(Figure 1-55)*.

Diversity

Diversity receivers are actually two receivers in one, because it turns out that having two different antenna orientations (a vertical-oriented whip antenna along with a horizontal one) or types (a whip antenna and a cloverleaf) can greatly improve the potential to receive signals. Diversity receivers will electronically select between the incoming signals and send the strongest one out to the monitor.

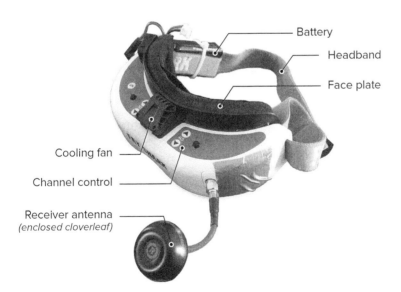

Figure 1-54. FPV goggles.

Figure 1-55.
(A) 5.8 GHz whip antenna and (B) cloverleaf antenna.

Antenna Placement

The placement and orientation of the video transmitter antenna can greatly affect the video signal. It is best when the antenna has a clear "view" on all sides. Carbon fiber structures can severely interfere with all types of signal. Finally, transmitters and receivers should be physically separated on the aircraft as much as possible in order to avoid bleed-over on other frequencies.

Directional Antennas

When clear video signals at long range are essential, a high-gain directional antenna may be used to focus receiving power toward the aircraft. The telemetry of some flight controllers may be used to control an aircraft-tracking antenna mount, which will move to point the directional antenna at the aircraft based on the GPS position and altitude received through the telemetry.

Selecting Components for a Multicopter

NOTE: This is an iterative process that may require multiple revisions. A digital spreadsheet may help to track specifications like weight and price for various components.

1. Determine what type of mission the aircraft is meant to perform. This will lead to the selection of a payload.

2. Determine any support equipment required for the selected payload. This will figure into the weight estimate and may necessitate other components, such as retractable landing gear.

3. Select an airframe. The more motors a multicopter has, the more likely that it will be able to safely survive a failure of one of those motors. This is appealing if an aircraft is meant to carry a big, expensive payload. However, having more arms at a given length may limit the propeller length that an airframe will accept; hence a coaxial configuration may be conducive to longer endurance while also keeping the aircraft relatively compact.

4. Select a flight controller based on mission requirements and supported airframe types.

5. Select an acceptable PDB based on size, mounting capability, and number of ports.

6. Research motors based on airframe manufacturer recommendations and propeller sizing.

7. Research ESCs based on maximum motor current requirements for a selected propeller size.

8. Research LiPo batteries based on the motor manufacturer's suggested cell count.

9. Produce a *weight estimate* by summing the weights of the following:

   a. Payload and airborne support equipment

   b. Airframe

   c. Flight controller and peripherals

   d. RC receiver

   e. PDB

   f. The heaviest motor option being considered* x the number of motors

   g. The heaviest ESC being considered* x the number of motors

   h. The heaviest battery being considered*
   Choose several acceptable options for the motor, ESC, and batteries, and use the heaviest of each in calculating this weight estimate.

10. Determine the thrust or lift required from each motor using the following formula:

    (2 x weight estimate) x 1.2 = maximum thrust required

    This is the maximum thrust required in order to achieve a hover with the throttle stick at its approximate midpoint while incorporating a 20% safety factor. This number is then used to determine the thrust required from each motor/propeller combination:

    maximum thrust required ÷ number of motors = maximum thrust required from an individual motor

11. Use the *maximum thrust required from an individual motor* as a minimum to select a motor/propeller combination based on manufacturer claims, which are usually found in the user documentation charts. Lower kV motors with longer propellers generally foster greater efficiency and longer endurance, but the greater mass of larger propellers may adversely affect maneuverability and response.

12. Once a motor/propeller combination is selected, a maximum current requirement for each motor can be found in the manufacturer's data or from thrust stand tests, along with a recommended LiPo cell count. These figures can in turn be used to select an ESC and battery, respectively.

13. Recalculate the weight estimate and thrust requirement figures with the selected components in order to verify that these components will function properly as part of the system as a whole.

Selecting Components for an Airplane

NOTE: This is an iterative process that may require multiple revisions. A digital spreadsheet may help to track specifications like weight and price for various components. It is also best to follow airframe manufacturer recommendations if available, especially for motors and servos.

1. Determine what type of mission the aircraft is meant to perform. This will lead to the selection of a payload.
2. Determine any support equipment required for the selected payload. This will figure into the weight estimate and may necessitate other components, such as retractable landing gear.
3. Select an airframe. For details, refer to the section regarding selection of a fixed-wing airframe, but chiefly consider the size of payload and support components as well as the aircraft launch and recovery method.
4. Select a flight controller based on mission requirements and supported airframe types.
5. Select an acceptable PDB based on size, mounting capability, and number of ports.
6. Research propellers based on airframe manufacturer recommendations and sizing requirements. Airplane propellers may be limited by ground clearance during landing and/or by clearance between the propeller blade tips and the physical structures of the airframe.
7. Research motors based on airframe manufacturer recommendations and the determined propeller sizing. A motor should be compatible with the motor mount and/or cowling and be capable of spinning the selected propeller at a speed that produces an acceptable amount of thrust.
8. Research ESCs based on maximum motor current requirements for a selected propeller size.
9. Research LiPo batteries based on the motor manufacturer's suggested cell count.

10. Produce a *weight estimate* by summing the weights of the following:

    a. Payload and airborne support equipment

    b. Airframe

    c. Flight controller and peripherals

    d. RC receiver

    e. PDB

    f. Heaviest weight of several acceptable motors* × Number of motors

    g. Heaviest weight of several acceptable ESCs* × Number of motors

    h. Heaviest weight of several acceptable batteries*
       Choose several acceptable options for the motor, ESC, and batteries, and use the heaviest of each in calculating this weight estimate.

11. Determine the thrust required from the motor(s) based on the weight of the aircraft. Fixed-wing propulsion is less straightforward than multicopters, as it can depend heavily on the drag on the aircraft and the type of maneuvers being executed. However, as a general rule, fixed-wing aircraft not required to execute aggressive maneuvers should be built with no less than a 1:4 thrust-to-weight ratio. This means that at their maximum output, the propulsion system is capable of generating about 115 grams of thrust for each pound of aircraft weight. Of course, the greater the thrust-to-weight ratio, the easier the aircraft will be to hand launch. Therefore, as long as it is practical (with regard to the physical sizing of the motor and propeller, and the amount of force that an aircraft is capable of enduring), it is almost always better to have more available thrust than is absolutely required.

12. Use the thrust required value as a minimum to select a motor/propeller combination based on manufacturer claims, which are usually found in the user documentation charts.

13. Once a motor/propeller combination is selected, a maximum current requirement for each motor can be found in the manufacturer's data, along with a recommended LiPo cell count. These figures can in turn be used to select an ESC and battery, respectively.

14. Recalculate the weight estimate and thrust requirement figures with the selected components in order to verify that these components will function properly as part of the system as a whole.

CHAPTER TWO

Aircraft Set Up

Assembly and Integration

EVERY AIRCRAFT ASSEMBLY will be different, depending on the airframe, flight controller, and payload. It is important to follow the manufacturers' instructions for assembly and integration; however, the following additional steps, described in detail in the following sections, can greatly improve performance:

1. Use fastener retention methods wherever possible
2. Use caution with electrical components
3. Plan component placement
4. Protect and secure connections
5. Carefully consider wiring and routing
6. Incorporate vibration mitigation
7. Consider upgrades, replacement, and maintenance

Fastener Retention Methods

Lock washers can be added on top of flat washers during initial assembly. Screws manufactured with patches of threadlocker can be ideal, eliminating the mess of liquid threadlocker and the need for lock washers. However, these patched fasteners can only be removed and reinstalled a handful of times before they should be replaced. Liquid threadlocker should be applied during final assembly, after the layout is finalized, and used where other retention methods are not possible, such as on countersink screws. When checking the tightness of these screws as part of regular preventative maintenance, it's important to remember that applying too much torque to the screws will break the bond of the threadlocker and necessitate reapplication. Fastener retention is especially important at critical junctures that are subject to vibrations, such as motor mounts and arm joints.

Using Caution with Electrical Components

Beyond the obvious need to use caution in order to avoid electrocution, mishandling electrical components can also be an expensive habit. Power supply voltages, especially from ESCs and programmable BECs, should be verified with a multimeter prior to connecting components. Components like BECs, video transmitters, and LEDs should be bench-tested with alligator clips prior to soldering permanently. Remember that the majority of payload components such as video transmitters, OSDs, and LEDs operate in the 12 V range, which means a BEC is required to avoid permanent damage if using a LiPo battery with four or more cells.

When wiring is complete, check for short circuits before connecting power to the aircraft. The easiest way to accomplish this is to use a multimeter to check continuity between the terminals of the battery connector on the aircraft. The multimeter may initially indicate continuity until the capacitors in the system energize and then should indicate an open circuit.

Planning Component Placement

You should begin to develop a plan for the mounting of components during assembly of the airframe. In some cases, certain components and wiring should be installed before the airframe is fully assembled. Consider these tips for proper mounting of components:

- *Flight Controller*—Mount centrally (at or near the CG) and orient correctly if the IMU and/or compass is internal. Isolate vibration as necessary.

- *External IMU*—Mount centrally, orient correctly, and isolate vibration. Some flight controller software will allow for an IMU (whether internal or external) to be mounted anywhere on the aircraft as long as the distance from the aircraft CG is specified during set up. However, mounting the IMU as close as possible to the CG will reduce maneuvering errors and may be necessary in some cases.

- *GPS/Compass*—This sensor is extremely sensitive to interference from the electrical system. Thus, the GPS/compass unit should be separated by distance from the main sources of interference, including the battery, PDB, and power wiring to the ESCs. On multicopters, this is accomplished by mounting the sensor on top of a mast. On most fixed-wing aircraft, the best mounting point for the GPS/compass unit is on the rear fuselage, where it is usually near only the wiring for the tail servos. The GPS receiver should have a clear view of the sky, unobstructed by the airframe structure, especially carbon fiber or metal.

- *Transmitters and Receivers*—Transmitters and receivers (especially their antennas) should be physically separated as much as possible to decrease bleed-over interference. This can be difficult on multirotors, as mounting these components on the arms may allow interference from the ESCs and power wiring. Mounting them on fixed landing gear and the outside of the central hub are usually the best options. Separating these components is usually easier on fixed-wing aircraft, allowing the RC receiver to be mounted in the fuselage with the telemetry unit and the video transmitter to be mounted on the underside of the wings. Purchasing SMA (sub-miniature version A) extension cables for these antennas can allow the telemetry unit and video transmitter themselves to be mounted in the fuselage while their antennas can be mounted in the wings. If a foam airplane is equipped with winglets, antennas may be mounted inside these structures to reduce the impact on airflow over the wings.

- *Airspeed Sensor*—It is important that the airspeed sensor pitot tube is exposed to clean airflow. Thus it is important that the pitot tube is neither directly in front of nor behind the propeller. Therefore, the pitot tube is best mounted on the leading edge of the wing or on a mast attached to the top or underside of the wing so that it is directed into the airflow. In addition, it is important to consider the placement of the airspeed sensor itself so that pressure tubing may be routed to the pitot tube.

- *Battery*—Some airframes will incorporate a battery-mounting plate, but in many cases it will be necessary to build one. A simple mounting plate consists of a flat, thin piece of wood, rigid plastic, or carbon fiber that is at least 1.5 times the length of the battery and is rigidly mounted to the airframe. Velcro or Dual Lock tape applied to the plate and the underside of the battery will prevent the battery from slipping on the mount, and one or two adjustable Velcro straps passing around the plate and battery will hold it in place.

Protecting and Securing Connections

Although electrical tape may be used to cover solder joints in a pinch, heat-shrink tubing performs much better and looks more professional. Of course, this requires the tubing to be prepared prior to soldering. Heat-shrink tubing can also be used to cover and secure connectors that are not disconnected on a regular basis. Connector coating, a type of insulating glue, may be used to cover contact solder connections, such as those on PDBs. However, once this is applied, it may make de-soldering difficult. The best solution for PDBs is to solder bullet connectors onto the connection terminals (if not already installed) and then cover the bullet connectors and contact pads with connector coating (insulating glue). Permanent servo connections should be secured with hot glue wherever possible.

Wiring and Routing

When it comes to wiring, the quickest, dirtiest way of getting an aircraft up and flying is to bundle up excess wire on board the aircraft. In the long run, however, eliminating this excess reduces the possibility of signal interference while also reducing the weight of the aircraft. ESCs and motors are the main culprits; unless they are made for a specific airframe, the manufacturer-provided connection lengths are rarely correct and will need to be cut and re-soldered. Investing in a crimping tool and servo connection pins for building custom-length servo connectors can be a good idea. If you are changing the length of the ESC-to-motor connections, it is important to cut all three wires to the same length to avoid affecting the timing of the AC pulses coming from the ESC.

It is also important to consider the routing of wiring through the aircraft. Whenever possible, avoid routing power wiring near the flight controller and/or its sensors to prevent interference. Bundles of servo and other data connections may be encased in braided sleeves to provide cleaner and more professional-looking wiring. Cable ties and adhesive-backed tie-down points may be used to secure wire routing.

Vibration Mitigation

In some cases, and especially in multicopters, vibrations from the motors can wreak havoc on the flight controller and other components. Ideally, the flight controller should make maneuvering calculations based on actual disturbances in attitude acceleration rather than signal noise caused by vibration. Many flight controllers employ signal filtering to reduce this noise, but physical vibration isolation reduces workload and improves performance in almost all systems. Most flight controllers recommend the use of thick, double-sided foam tape for mounting of the flight controller and IMU. If more thorough isolation is required, then consider building a vibration-isolated mount using special foam or gel grommets.

Vibrations can also severely impact the system's ability to gather clear footage for professional video applications. Thus, vibration isolation should be installed between the aircraft and camera mounts. Pillow ball mounts, loaded in compression, are an affordable and easy way of accomplishing this, while wire rope isolators usually provide better isolation for heavy payloads and may be mounted in various orientations, but are generally more expensive (*Figure 2-1*). In either case, it is important to select isolators that are specifically tuned to carry the proper weight.

Stiff wiring can transmit vibrations between components. While stiff Teflon-insulated wire can be ideal for feeding runs of wire though tight spaces, more flexible, silicone-insulated wire should be used for any wiring connecting to the flight controller, IMU, or

Pillow/ball isolators

A

B

Pillow/ball isolator   Wire rope isolator

Figure 2-1. Vibration isolators: (A) payload vibration isolation mount; (B) pillow/ball isolator and wire rope isolator.

camera mount. Standard three-wire servo connections usually are sufficiently flexible, but other wiring may be questionable. One advantage of isolated flight controller mounting plates and camera mounts is that wiring may be tied down to these plates before passing to the mounted components, reducing the level of vibrations transmitted to them.

Attempting to reduce the vibration at its source can also be beneficial. Most high-quality motors are generally balanced at the factory, while lower-quality, cheaper motors may not be. This is an important point to consider, as attempting to balance a motor by hand is difficult, risky, and arguably not worth the effort. Propellers, on the other hand, may be balanced relatively easily using a prop balancing device. (See Chapter 1 for more details on propeller balancing.)

Upgrades, Replacement, and Maintenance

Initial assembly can be the best time to install upgrades or install the necessary provisions for future use. Motors and ESCs tend to be the most often replaced components on multicopters, so specific connector placement on inboard and outboard wires can allow these components to be more easily removed if necessary. Wiring to allow LEDs to be installed on the arms is more easily routed while the arms or wings are disassembled or not installed. Of course, these wires must be properly capped off if not being used immediately. Adding colored LEDs to the arms of a multicopter or the wing tips of an airplane can be a simple way to improve visibility and make the aircraft look more professional. Finally, if providing regulated 12 V power from a BEC, adding extra output connections to allow for the addition of components in the future is recommended.

Information Common to Multicopters and Airplanes

Standard RC Connections

Not surprisingly, many of the connections in small autonomous aircraft—including those between the RC receiver, flight controller, and maneuvering controls—are made with standard RC connectors that have been used for decades in RC flying. These connectors, also referred to as servo connectors, consist of three terminals carrying signals (usually PWM), power (usually 5 volts), and ground for both. These connector cables are usually built using thin-gauge wire with colored insulation to denote the purpose of each wire *(Figure 2-2A)*. Yellow, red, and black; orange, red, and brown; or white, red, and black may be used to denote signal, power, and ground, respectively.

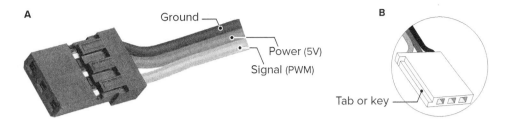

Figure 2-2. (A) A standard RC or servo connection. (B) Futaba-style connector. *(left: istock.com/digitalr)*

/ SELECTING CONNECTORS

Plastic connector housings vary between manufacturers. Most notably, those designed to interface with Futaba systems include tabs or keys on the side of the signal wire (as shown in *Figure 2-2B*), designed to prevent a backwards connection when interfacing with other Futaba components. However, this tab may need to be trimmed away in order to properly connect to certain components. This requires pilots to be aware of the pin out assignments on such components. Selecting or requesting proper connectors can also generate some confusion with regard to gender, as the plastic connector housings may be considered male while the crimps within the housing are actually female.

/ CONNECTION CONSIDERATIONS

The signal and power wires may be considered optional, whereas the ground connection is required whenever a connection is made. Servos require all three wires providing the necessary 5 volts of power and the PWM control signal. ESCs, however, require only signal and ground because they are provided with higher voltage power through separate, thick-gauge connections from the PDB. Therefore, unless the ESC is equipped with an internal BEC (as in a single-motor airplane), the power wire in the RC connection should be de-pinned and capped using heat shrink tubing. This will reduce the likelihood of electrical interference over this connection. Some video systems may also use servo connectors, in many cases only requiring the signal and ground connections, with the video being carried on the signal wire.

Motor and ESC Set Up

Testing of the motors is, in many cases, the culmination of constructing a multicopter and an essential part of the pre-flight testing process.

/ ESC CALIBRATION

As mentioned in the ESC section, proper calibration of the ESCs is critical, especially for multicopters. Improper calibration can lead to unstable flight, problems with tuning, and even a crash. ESC calibration is also important on fixed-wing aircraft, especially those having multiple engines.

The following are required for the calibration process:

- ESC(s)
- Motors
- RC receiver
- RC transmitter
- Power source for the ESC (flight battery)
- Power source for the RC receiver (if the ESC does not contain a BEC)
- Flight controller (with simultaneous calibration capability) or appropriate multiple output harness (recommended)

One-by-One Calibration

Follow these steps if the flight controller is not capable of all-at-once calibration, or if you want to observe each motor separately. This procedure is also applicable when only one ESC requires calibration, as in most fixed-wing aircraft.

Note: Before beginning this process, consult the ESC's user documentation and verify that the ESC can in fact be calibrated, and review the calibration process, if applicable.

1. Prepare ESCs and motors with appropriate connectors (bullet-type connectors are recommended) in order to connect the ESC to the power source and the motor to the ESC. Soldering may be required. A special adapter may also be required in order to connect the ESC directly to a flight battery or power source for calibration.

2. Securely mount the motor to its mount, appropriate multicopter arm, or a calibration test fixture that will allow it to spin freely during testing. Verify that the motor is secure.

3. Connect the motor to the ESC. The resulting spin direction may not initially be correct, but this will be checked during the calibration process. ***Do not install the propeller.***

4. For a multirotor, number the motor and ESC and note the intended spin direction for this motor position.

5. Connect the servo command input lead directly to the throttle channel port on the RC receiver (usually channel 3).

6. Perform a final check to ensure that the motors are secure, free of debris, and capable of spinning freely. Also ensure that all electrical connections are secure and safe.

7. Power on the RC transmitter and configure it appropriately to place the ESCs in calibration. (Usually this involves placing the throttle stick in its maximum position while power is applied to the ESC. Consult the ESC's user documentation for details.)

8. If this ESC contains an internal BEC, the RC receiver will be powered through its connection to the ESC when power is connected to it. If not, a separate power source will be required to power the RC receiver (usually a 1–2S LiPo battery with a servo connector). Connect this RC receiver power source and confirm that it is powered on, then connect the other power source to the ESC.

9. Once power is connected to the system, the motor may begin to twitch but should not move significantly. This is normal. The ESC may also emit a tone indicating that the ESC is in calibration mode. If this tone is anticipated but not observed, then the throttle channel may be reversed. In this case, disconnect all power, make the appropriate change on the RC transmitter, and return to Step 7.

10. Once the ESC calibration mode is verified, complete the calibration procedure described in the ESC's user documentation. This usually involves moving the throttle stick to its minimum and maximum positions.

11. Most ESCs will emit a tone once the calibration process is complete. At this point, the ESC is usually armed, meaning the motor will spin in direct response to any movements of the stick. This is a good opportunity to check that the motor spins up properly and verify that the spin direction is correct. (See the Checking Motor Spin Directions section later in this chapter.)

12. If the spin direction of a motor must be reversed, follow the motor reversal procedure described later in this chapter.

13. Disconnect all power from the aircraft, power down the RC transmitter, and repeat this process for all motors, as necessary.

All-At-Once Calibration (Multicopters)

Follow these steps if using the all-at-once calibration feature of a flight controller. This procedure is the most efficient way to ensure that multiple ESCs are calibrated identically, and thus is the recommended method for multicopters.

Note: Before beginning this process, consult the ESC's user documentation and verify that the ESC can in fact be calibrated, and review the calibration process, if applicable.

1. Prepare ESCs and motors with appropriate connectors (bullet-type connectors are recommended) in order to connect the ESCs to the PDB and the motors to the ESC. Soldering will most likely be required.

2. Assemble the airframe with:
   - PDB mounted.
   - PMU power output connector connected to the PDB and the flight controller lead connected to the appropriate terminal on the flight controller.
   - Flight controller mounted.

- ESC power wires routed to the PDB and connected to appropriate terminals.
- Motors securely mounted. Verify that the motor is secure. ***Do not install the propellers.***
- ESC-to-motor wires connected but fully accessible in case the motor spin direction must be reversed. It is also preferable that the ESC itself be fully accessible at this time.
- RC receiver and sensors connected to the flight controller correctly. *Note:* The sensors should not be utilized by the flight controller during the calibration process, so they do not need to be permanently mounted at this time. Connecting them only serves to avoid power-on errors that may prevent the flight controller from entering calibration mode.
- All wires routed and secured so that they do not impede the motors from spinning freely.

3. Perform a final check to ensure that the motors are secure, free of debris, and capable of spinning freely. Also ensure that all electrical connections are secure and safe.
   Tip: Because at this point almost all of the high-value components are installed, it is advisable to have another person verify that all construction and electrical connections are safe.

4. Power on the RC transmitter and configure it appropriately to place the flight controller in all-at-once calibration mode. (This usually involves placing the throttle stick in its maximum position when powering on the aircraft.) Consult the flight controller's user documentation for details.

5. Place the flight controller in all-at-once calibration mode and verify.

6. Place the ESCs in calibration mode. This will most likely involve leaving the throttle stick on the RC transmitter in its maximum position while applying power to the aircraft and in turn to the ESCs. (Consult the ESC's user documentation for details.)

7. Once power is connected to the system, the motors may begin to twitch but should not move significantly. This is normal. The ESCs may also emit a tone indicating that the ESCs are in calibration mode.

8. Once ESC calibration mode is verified, complete the calibration procedure described in the ESC's user documentation. This usually involves moving the throttle stick to its minimum and maximum positions.

9. Most ESCs will emit a tone indicating when the calibration process is complete. At this point, the ESCs are usually armed, meaning that the motor will spin in direct response to any movements of the stick. This is a good opportunity to check that all motors spin up properly and at equal speed for a given throttle

setting. Also verify that the spin direction for each motor is correct, as described in the next section.

10. If the spin direction of any motors must be reversed, follow the motor reversal procedure described in the next section.

11. Disconnect all power from the aircraft and power down the RC transmitter.

/ CHECKING MOTOR SPIN DIRECTIONS

It is crucial to verify the spin direction of all motors during the initial set up and whenever changes are made to an ESC/motor combination. In some cases, the spin direction of a moving motor may be observed visually, especially when it slows to a stop. But in other cases, especially with inrunner motors, this is not possible, and a short piece of light string taped to the motor shaft can be used to verify the spin direction by observing the direction that the string spools around the shaft when rotating.

Motor Reversal Procedure

If the spin direction of a brushless motor must be reversed:

1. Disconnect all power from the aircraft.

2. Ensure that all propellers are off of the motors.

3. Swap any two of the three ESC-to-motor connection wires on the motor(s) that must be reversed.

4. Power on the RC transmitter.

5. Set the throttle stick on the RC transmitter to its minimum position.

6. Reconnect power to the aircraft.

7. Run up the throttle and verify that all spin directions are now correct.

Multicopter Set Up

Before Powering On

1. Install mission control software on the interface device.

2. Perform a preflight inspection as appropriate. This serves as an opportunity to check connections and linkages before powering on.

3. Check continuity between the power and ground leads of the battery connector on the aircraft using a multimeter. This is a rudimentary way of checking that there are no short circuits within the aircraft wiring. When connected to the flight battery terminals, the multimeter may momentarily indicate continuity due to the capacitors within the system but should indicate an open circuit after a few seconds. Otherwise, there may be a short circuit in the system.

4. Remove all propellers. In the event that the RC transmitter channels are improperly assigned, the throttle channel is reversed, or the throttle channel is connected to the wrong RC receiver output port, the motor(s) may spin unexpectedly.

Set-Up Process

1. **Power on the RC transmitter, power on the aircraft, and bind the RC receiver to the transmitter.**
This may require inserting a bind plug into a special port on the receiver and/or pressing a button on the RC transmitter before or during power up. Consult your RC transmitter and receiver documentation for specifics. It is important that the RC receiver is easily accessible during this process.

2. **Install the appropriate multicopter firmware on the flight controller.**
This will normally require that the aircraft be powered on and connected directly via USB cable to a laptop running configuration software. It is prudent to use a fully charged aircraft battery and a laptop power supply, as an interruption during firmware updates may be fatal to the flight controller. Next, select the appropriate frame type based on the number of motors and orientation.

3. **Verify the ability to connect to the aircraft via the wireless telemetry link.**
Observing the artificial horizon within the mission control software is the simplest way to verify a successful connection, as movements of the aircraft will be reflected here.

4. **Calibrate sensors:**
   a. *IMU*—Most configuration software requires the user to specify the mounting orientation of the IMU within the aircraft. After the orientation is selected, the IMU may be calibrated, which usually requires the user to place the aircraft in several commanded orientations (including a level surface in order to capture a straight-and-level orientation).
   b. *Compass/Magnetometer*—Once the orientation of the compass is selected in the flight control software, it is normally calibrated by rotating the aircraft about all of its axes while in the compass calibration mode. The "compass calibration dance" may be performed by holding the aircraft in a straight-and-level orientation and slowly rotating your body 360 degrees, and then repeating this rotation while holding the aircraft in other orientations such as nose up, nose down, right wing up, left wing up, and inverted. The purpose of this calibration is to tune the compass unit to local magnetic fields within the operating area (which may differ substantially from location to location due to magnetic bodies and/or normal geographic declination) as well as to magnetic fields within the aircraft. Therefore, it is

important to perform compass calibrations with the aircraft in the configuration in which it will operate and with all metallic components in place. Note that sources of interference such as cell phones may adversely affect calibrations.

c. *Power Management Unit*—Some configuration software allows the user to calibrate the power management unit. This may be done by simply entering the correct voltage of the battery, measured using a battery cell checker.

5. **Verify RC transmitter channel assignment and directions by observing the response of the appropriate flight controller software displays. Reassign and/or reverse as necessary.**

Almost all flight controller GCS software includes a display for viewing the RC inputs observed by the flight controller. In many cases, this part of the software also incorporates a means of calibrating the flight controller to the end points of these input channels.

In almost all cases, multicopter flight controllers are designed to receive RC control inputs from an RC transmitter in the default airplane channel configuration shown in Table 2-1. However, in most RC transmitters, these assignments may be altered as necessary (for example, to allow better left-handed control).

Table 2-1. RC Transmitter Default Channel Configuration (Mode 2)

CHANNEL	MANEUVER	STICK	AXIS
1	Roll	Right	Left-Right Axis
2	Pitch	Right	Up-Down Axis
3	Thrust	Left	Up-Down Axis
4	Yaw	Left	Left-Right Axis

6. **Calibrate the ESCs.**

ESC calibration programs the throttle end points and, if applicable, the throttle curve to the ESCs. This is especially important in multicopters, which incorporate multiple motors, in order to program the motors to output the same RPM at a given throttle setting during a hover. ESC calibration usually requires placing the throttle control stick in the full throttle position while powering on the aircraft, then reducing the throttle control stick to its minimum position. Consult the ESC manufacturer's documentation for details. Once again, it is important for safety reasons to perform ESC calibration with the propellers off.

Some flight controllers allow for a special ESC calibration mode that allows all of the ESCs to be calibrated identically at once. An alternative is to purchase or build a cable that splits the output from the RC receiver throttle channel to multiple ports.

7. **Perform a motor test.**

Most flight controller software allows for one-by-one motor testing. This will verify that each motor is connected to the correct output port on the flight controller. This is also an opportunity to verify that each motor is spinning in the correct direction. Remember, to reverse the spin direction of a motor, simply swap any two of the three connections between the ESC and the motor. Both the output port and spin direction for each motor are dictated by motor configurations specified in the flight controller documentation.

8. **Perform a stabilization and control check.**

First, it is important to verify that the IMU has been properly mounted, set up, and calibrated. You may easily verify this using the artificial horizon displayed in the GCS software. If the indication of the artificial horizon is incorrect, either the IMU is not oriented correctly, or an IMU mounting parameter must be changed in the flight controller software to reflect the actual mounting of the IMU.

The stabilization and control check serves two main purposes: (1) To verify that RC commands are being successfully conveyed to the motors and (2) to verify that the aircraft is capable of stabilizing itself based on motor outputs. For example, if a roll to the left is commanded, then the motors on the left side of the aircraft should be observed to decrease RPM while those on the right side should increase RPM. When this roll command is released, the opposite reaction should be observed in order to return the aircraft to level flight. This check may be accomplished in several ways:

a. *With the Propellers Off—Software Output Check:* Some flight controller software is capable of displaying the signal being sent to each of the output ports of the flight controller. If the motors are connected correctly, by providing RC inputs and disturbing the aircraft from level attitude, this check should provide some indication as to whether the aircraft will properly maneuver and stabilize. However, this method will not catch a motor malfunction or a calibration error.

b. *With Propellers On—Hand Check:* This method should only be used for small aircraft and only if it can be performed safely. Securely hold the aircraft while remaining clear of the propeller arcs. This usually requires holding the aircraft overhead. Have an assistant arm the aircraft, raise the throttle to about 50%, and then provide pitch and roll RC inputs while verbally calling out those inputs. Verify by feel that the motors are responding correctly based on the given RC inputs. Next, manually disturb the aircraft from level attitude, and the thrust from the motors should tend to resist this disturbance in order to return to a level state.

   c. *Strap-Down Check:* If an aircraft is too large to safely perform a hand check with the propellers on, it may be possible to perform a similar check by strapping the aircraft to a heavy table or other secure structure. In this case, it is essential that the airframe is solidly assembled, the straps are secure, and the straps do not interfere with the propeller arcs. While providing pitch and roll RC inputs with the throttle at approximately 50% power, a small amount of flex should be observed in the arm and airframe, which will indicate the maneuvering response of the motors. However, this method does not provide the ability to verify stabilization.

      A strap-down test may also be useful for determining the effect, if any, of the magnetic interference from the ESCs and motors on the compass unit. Before beginning the strap-down test, note the heading of the aircraft indicated by the flight control software. As the motors are spun up, watch for any change in the indicated heading. If it varies by more than ±3 degrees, consider raising the compass unit to increase the distance from sources of interference or installing electromagnetic shielding material below the unit. Some flight controllers will provide a means of measuring this interference during strap-down tests along with suggestions of acceptable levels.

Airplane Set Up

Before Powering On

1. Install mission control software on the interface device.

2. Perform a preflight inspection as appropriate. This serves as an opportunity to check connections and linkages before powering on.

3. Check continuity between the power and ground leads of the battery connector on the aircraft. This is a rudimentary way of checking that no short circuits exist within the aircraft wiring. When connected to the flight battery terminals, the multimeter may momentarily indicate continuity due to the capacitors within the system but should indicate an open circuit after a few seconds. Otherwise, there may be a short circuit in the system.

4. Remove all propellers. In the event that the RC transmitter channels are improperly assigned, the throttle channel is reversed, or the throttle channel is connected to the wrong RC receiver output port, the motor(s) may spin unexpectedly.

Set-Up Process

1. **Power on the RC transmitter, power on the aircraft, and bind the RC receiver to the transmitter.**
   This may require inserting a bind plug into a special port on the receiver and/or pressing a button on the RC transmitter before or during power up. Consult your RC transmitter and receiver documentation for specifics. It is important that the RC receiver is easily accessible during this process.

2. **Install the appropriate fixed-wing firmware on the flight controller.**
   This will normally require that the aircraft be powered on and connected directly via USB cable to a laptop running configuration software. It is prudent to use a fully charged aircraft battery and a laptop power supply, because an interruption during firmware updates may be fatal to the flight controller.

3. **Verify the ability to connect to the aircraft via the wireless telemetry link.**
   Observing the artificial horizon within the mission control software is the simplest way to verify a successful connection, as movements of the aircraft will be reflected here.

4. **Calibrate sensors:**

   a. *IMU*—Most configuration software requires the user to specify the mounting orientation of the IMU within the aircraft. After the orientation is selected, the IMU may be calibrated, which usually requires the user to place the aircraft in several commanded orientations (including a level surface in order to capture a straight-and-level orientation).

   b. *Compass/Magnetometer*—Once the orientation of the compass is selected in the flight control software, it is normally calibrated by rotating the aircraft about all of its axes while in the compass calibration mode. The "compass calibration dance" may be performed by holding the aircraft in a straight-and-level orientation and slowly rotating your body 360 degrees, and then repeating this rotation while holding the aircraft in other orientations such as nose up, nose down, right wing up, left wing up, and inverted. The purpose of this calibration is to tune the compass unit to local magnetic fields within the operating area (which may differ substantially from location to location due to magnetic bodies and/or normal geographic declination) as well as to magnetic fields within the aircraft. Therefore, it is important to perform compass calibrations with the aircraft in the configuration in which it will operate and with all metallic components in place. It should be noted that sources of interference such as cell phones may adversely affect calibrations.

c. *Power Management Unit*—Some configuration software allows the user to calibrate the power management unit. This is done by simply entering the correct voltage of the battery, measured using a battery cell checker.

d. *Airspeed Module*—Airspeed modules are normally calibrated by zeroing them while the aircraft is at rest. This should be performed with the inlet of the pitot tube covered with a fitted sleeve or your hand in such a way that the movement of air around the inlet does not affect the calibration. However, the inlet should not be sealed off completely (for example, by covering it with a fingertip) as this can cause pressure buildup and affect the result. Proper calibration may be checked by verifying that the airspeed indicated within the mission control software is approximately zero while the aircraft is at rest, and that a positive airspeed is indicated when air is gently blown into the inlet of the pitot tube. If the airspeed indicates negative, then the pressure lines leading from the pitot tube to the airspeed sensor module have likely been reversed. When you stop blowing into the pitot tube, the indicated airspeed should return to approximately zero. Sealing the front opening of a pitot tube with a fingertip may be used to check for leaks in the system. While this opening is tightly covered, you should see the airspeed reading rise as pressure builds, eventually leveling off. This airspeed reading should return to zero when the finger is removed. If airspeed is not maintained, this may be an indication of a leak between the pitot tube and the airspeed sensor.

5. **Verify your ability to take manual control of the aircraft, either using an external MUX or a manual mode of the flight controller.**
This will also verify the functionality of the switch on the RC transmitter that controls the flight controller's flight mode. Reassign and/or reverse this channel as necessary.

6. **Verify the appropriate mixing is selected.**
If using an external MUX: The RC transmitter should be programmed so that the same switch that controls the MUX also controls the aileron and/or V-tail mixing. If correctly set up, the appropriate mixing should be in effect when the RC receiver has authority and removed when the flight controller has authority. The appropriate mixing should also be selected in the flight controller.
If not using an external MUX: Mixing should be programmed in the flight controller and not in the RC transmitter.

7. **Verify RC transmitter channel assignment by observing the response of the appropriate control surface(s) and motor(s). Reassign as necessary.**
If using an external MUX: Verify these assignments in both MUX settings, thus verifying the channel assignments of both the RC transmitter and the flight controller.

If not using an external MUX: Verify these assignments while the flight controller is in a manual flight mode, thus verifying the channel assignments of both the RC transmitter and the flight controller.

8. **Verify RC channel directions by observing the deflection direction of the corresponding control surface(s) and motor(s). Reverse channels through the RC transmitter as necessary.**
   The correct control surface and motor responses to control inputs are shown in Table 2-2.

Table 2-2. Correct Control Surface or Motor Response to Control Inputs

	CONTROL INPUT	CONTROL SURFACE OR MOTOR RESPONSE
Ailerons	Stick left (left roll) Stick right (right roll)	Left aileron up, right aileron down Left aileron down, right aileron up
Elevator	Stick up (nose down pitch) Stick down (nose up pitch)	Elevator down Elevator up
Throttle	Stick up Stick down	Full throttle Motor(s) off
Rudder	Stick left (yaw left) Stick right (yaw right)	Rudder left Rudder right

If using an external MUX: Verify these channel directions in both MUX settings, thus verifying the channel directions of both the RC transmitter and the flight controller.

If not using an external MUX: Verify these channel directions while the flight controller is in a manual flight mode, thus verifying the channel directions of both the RC transmitter and the flight controller.

9. **Verify the neutral positions of each of the control surfaces.**
   The neutral position refers to the servo's displacement of a control surface when the corresponding RC transmitter control stick is released to its center or neutral position. In theory, the neutral position should not produce any maneuvering, as in calm, straight-and-level flight. Unless otherwise noted by the aircraft manufacturer, the neutral position of a control surface should be in line with the trailing edge of the lifting body to which it is attached. Preferably, this should be adjusted mechanically rather than using the subtrims of the RC transmitter, as this approach will accommodate both single and two-servo aileron control configurations and allows for an easier transition between RC receiver and flight controller authority. Therefore, threaded control linkage rods used in conjunction with adjustable clevis or ball links are preferable for most applications, allowing relatively easy adjustment of linkage lengths.

   If using an external MUX: First, verify the neutral positions of the control surfaces while the RC receiver has authority. Next, verify that these neutral positions do not change when switching over to flight controller authority. This may require adjustment of the flight controller neutral point parameters, which are usually set as PWM values. A device called a servo tester may be useful in this process, measuring the PWM output on a given RC receiver channel. This value may then be entered into the flight controller so that switching of the MUX does not affect the PWM value seen by the appropriate maneuvering control.

10. **Verify the control surface throws.**
The term "throw" refers to the maximum deflection of an individual control surface in either direction. Unless specified by the aircraft manufacturer, it is important to verify that the upward and downward throws of one aileron match the upward and downward throws of the other, thus providing for balanced roll in both directions. Adjustment of the throws should be primarily accomplished mechanically by adjusting the servo horn and/or the linkage length but may also be adjusted by the channel end points on the RC transmitter. You may also choose to adjust the channel end points of any of the control surfaces in order to improve handling as dictated by flight testing and personal preference.

If using an external MUX: First verify the throws of the control surfaces while the RC receiver has authority. Next, verify that these throws do not change when switching over to flight controller authority. This may require adjustment of the flight controller channel end-point parameters, which are usually set as PWM values. Once again, a servo tester may be used to measure the PWM output on a given RC receiver channel. This value may then be entered into the flight controller so that switching of the MUX does not affect the PWM value that is seen by the appropriate maneuvering control.

11. **Set up the flaps.**
The flaps are generally assigned to a two- or three-position switch on the RC receiver, which allows for flaps to be placed at the neutral position (no deflection), maximum deflection, and possibly an intermediate deflection. Some aircraft manufacturers will provide recommendations for proper flap deflection angles during landing and/or takeoff. Maximum deflection is usually not more than 30 degrees.

It is important to verify that both flaps deflect downward simultaneously, that the neutral position aligns the trailing edge of the flaps with that of the wing (similar to the ailerons), and that the servo throws allow the flaps on either side of the wing to deflect the same distance for a given setting. Both the neutral point and the throws are best adjusted mechanically (as with the control surfaces).

Flight controllers that support flap deployment require editing parameters regarding automatic flap deployment during takeoff and landing. Using flaps during autonomous flight is not recommended if the flight controller does not support this function.

If using an external MUX: First verify the flap directions, neutral positions, and throws while the RC receiver has authority. Then verify that these settings do not change when switching over to flight controller authority. This may require editing of the flight controller flap parameter. Once again, a servo tester may be helpful.

Note that the deployment of flaps will likely result in a pitch up tendency, which may be counteracted through mixing of the pitch channel in conjunction with the flap switch.

12. **Program the ESC(s) (if applicable).**
Some ESCs require programming either through specific RC transmitter stick inputs or through external means, such as a programming card or cable. The most important programming setting, beyond selection of battery type if necessary, is the braking function. Turning braking on prevents the propeller from spinning in the wind (windmilling) when the motor is off. This is preferred for belly landing aircraft as it prevents a windmilling propeller from digging into the ground during landing, which may cause damage. Braking may also be beneficial in powered gliders, which commonly use hinged propellers that fold back against the fuselage when the motor is off.

13. **Calibrate the ESC(s).**
ESC calibration programs the throttle end points and, if applicable, the throttle curve to the ESC(s). This is especially important if using multiple motors to program them to output the same RPM at a given throttle setting. ESC calibration usually requires placing the throttle control stick in the full throttle position while powering on the aircraft, then reducing the throttle control stick to its minimum position. Consult the ESC manufacturer's documentation for details. Once again, it is important for safety reasons to perform ESC calibration with the propellers off.

If using an external MUX: Calibrate the ESC(s) while the RC receiver has authority.

If not using an external MUX: It is usually best to connect the ESC PWM input directly into the RC receiver throttle output port while calibrating the ESC.

14. **Verify control surface responses while under flight controller authority and in a stabilize flight mode.**
This is the final verification that the flight controller is set up correctly. First, it is important to verify that the IMU has been properly mounted, set up, and calibrated. This may be easily observed using the artificial horizon displayed in the GCS software. If the indication of the artificial horizon is incorrect, either the IMU is not oriented correctly, or an IMU mounting parameter must be changed in the flight controller software to reflect the actual mounting of the IMU.

Then, while in a stabilize flight mode, the control surfaces should deflect in order to maintain straight-and-level flight when a disturbance is introduced. Changing the attitude of the aircraft by hand should cause the control surfaces to react by producing a maneuver in the opposite direction, as shown in Table 2-3.

Table 2-3. Control Surface Reactions to Disturbances While in Stabilize Flight Mode

DISTURBANCE	REACTION	DISTURBANCE	REACTION
Left wing up	Left aileron up / right aileron down	Nose up	Elevator down
Right wing up	Left aileron up / right aileron down	Nose down	Elevator up

15. **Set up aircraft failsafe conditions and actions.**

    a. Select battery voltage (and capacity, if applicable) levels that will trigger failsafe.

    b. Select the action to be executed in the event of a battery failsafe condition.
    Recommended: Return Home and Land

    c. Select the RC Link Loss delay and/or enabling.

    d. Select the action to be executed in the event of an RC Link Loss failsafe condition.
    Recommended: Return Home, Loiter, and Land

    e. Select the Telemetry Link Loss delay and/or enabling.

    f. Select the action to be executed in the event of a Telemetry Link Loss failsafe condition.
    Recommended: Return Home, Loiter, and Land

    g. Select the action to be executed in the event of a Geofence breach.
    Recommended: Return Home, Loiter, and Land

    h. Select the action to be executed in the event of a loss of GPS lock.
    Recommended: Land Now

16. **Test failsafe responses (as possible):**

    a. With the aircraft active, turn off the RC transmitter and observe the RC link loss failsafe condition in the mission control software (after the appropriate delay) and observe the appropriate response of aircraft control surfaces. Power on the RC transmitter and verify the ability to regain manual control of the aircraft.

    b. With the aircraft active, disconnect the ground telemetry unit from the interface device and observe the appropriate response of the aircraft control surfaces. Reconnect the telemetry unit and verify the ability to reacquire the aircraft.

    c. Using an adjustable AC-to-DC power supply and appropriate adapter, reduce the input voltage below the failsafe voltage; observe the RC battery failsafe condition and observe the appropriate response of the aircraft control surfaces.

CHAPTER THREE

Flight Controller Fundamentals

Common Flight Modes

MANY FLIGHT CONTROLLER SYSTEMS provide various flight modes that are meant to maintain certain parameters, in some cases accepting inputs from the operator to make the aircraft easier and safer to fly. The proper functioning of these flight modes is heavily dependent on the proportional-integral-derivative (PID) algorithm tuning and parameter setting of the autopilot.

Stabilize (Fixed and Rotor Wing)

In a Stabilize mode, the aircraft attempts to maintain straight-and-level flight (or hover, in the case of rotor-wing aircraft). Stabilize modes commonly use an attitude control scheme allowing the operator to directly command the pitch and roll of the aircraft rather than the rate(s) of change of these attitudes as with RC aircraft. Of course, for this attitude scheme to work, the flight controller must be able to monitor the attitude of the aircraft, which is the function of the IMU. The flight controller will then use PID loops to dynamically maintain the attitude commanded by the operator, thus stabilizing the aircraft.

Most flight controllers will allow the operator to specify maximum pitch and roll values for the aircraft equating to the pitch and roll values that will be commanded when the RC transmitter sticks are deflected to their maximum position. For rotor-wing aircraft, ±30 degrees in both pitch and roll is usually appropriate. For fixed-wing aircraft, ±30 degrees in roll and ±10 degrees in pitch is usually a good place to start. This attitude-limiting function helps to limit the aggressiveness of maneuvers and reduce the likelihood of the aircraft becoming uncontrollable, such as in the case of a stall or spin. Due to the attitude stabilization and limitations, Stabilize mode is commonly used when manual control of the aircraft via the RC transmitter is necessary or when learning to fly with the transmitter.

One shortcoming of Stabilize mode, particularly for rotor-wing aircraft, is that it is not governed by GPS position. While in a hover (RC transmitter stick neutral), the aircraft will maintain a level orientation but may still be pushed out of position by wind. In another example, if an operator commands full right roll for one-half second and then releases the control stick to the neutral position, the aircraft will roll to its specified roll limit angle for one-half second and then, once the stick is released, return to a level-roll orientation. The aircraft will continue to move in the direction of the roll, carrying the velocity gained by the brief roll command, but it will eventually come to a stop and hover if no other control inputs are received. This behavior can be counteracted using a GPS mode as described later in this chapter.

Auto (Fixed and Rotor Wing)

Autonomous or Auto flight mode commands the autopilot to execute whatever flight plan is stored within its memory. This turns control of the aircraft over to the autopilot; however, the operator may command the aircraft into another flight mode, either through telemetry or RC, at any time and regain control.

Return to Home (RTH) (Fixed and Rotor Wing)

Return to Home (RTH) mode is another flight mode that transfers control of the aircraft to the autopilot. When the aircraft enters this mode, the autopilot commands a climb to a predetermined altitude in order to avoid any obstacles. The aircraft will then fly to its home position, which is either the position specified as part of the flight plan or the point where the aircraft was first armed. A rotor-wing aircraft may be preprogrammed to begin a descent to a specified altitude once it reaches its home position. This final altitude may also be set to zero (above the ground) in order to execute an automatic landing. Fixed-wing aircraft, upon reaching their home position, will generally circle over that position until a new command is received from the operator, but these aircraft may also be programmed to execute a Land Now maneuver.

Land Now (Fixed and Rotor Wing)

Land Now mode, if available for a fixed-wing aircraft, will usually command it to begin a descending spiral at its current position, usually bound by a specified spiral radius and descent rate. The aircraft will continue until coming to rest on the ground. This mode is not recommended for fixed-wing aircraft except in extreme circumstances, such as to prevent an emergency that may not be covered by a failsafe contingency. The more traditional mode for landing an airplane, based on a sloped approach path to a runway, is typically only available as part of an autonomous flight plan.

In a rotor-wing platform, Land Now will command the aircraft into a descent at the predetermined landing descent rate while maintaining GPS position. The aircraft will continue to descend, landing similarly to when it's in RTH mode. It should be noted that some flight controllers will decrease the descent rate of a rotor-wing aircraft when approaching the ground (a so-called final descent rate) while also limiting the attitude range of the aircraft in an attempt to touch down in an orientation as close to level as possible. However, limiting the attitude range may deprioritize position accuracy and cause the aircraft to be pushed off target in breezy conditions.

Aircraft-Specific Flight Modes

MANY FLIGHT CONTROLLERS will provide a means of assisting the operator in controlling the aircraft while flying manually via the RC transmitter. These modes are dependent on the type of aircraft.

Augmented Rotor-Wing Control Modes

Some flight controllers will provide flight modes intended to assist the operator while flying a rotor-wing aircraft in manual modes. In general, these modes provide better control of the aircraft's position and, in some cases, are not affected by the heading orientation. Augmented modes for rotor-wing aircraft may include Climb and Descent Control, GPS, Grid, and Radius.

/ CLIMB AND DESCENT CONTROL

Regardless of the flight mode selected, a flight controller in a rotor-wing aircraft will usually attempt to regulate vertical speed (the rate of climb or descent). This vertical speed is controlled via the throttle stick commanding changes in collective thrust output. A neutral throttle position (50%) usually will command the flight controller to maintain a vertical speed of 0 (level flight with altitude maintained). Note that many sensors can factor into the flight controller's calculation of vertical speed including the IMU, barometer, 3D GPS position, and AGL range sensor at low altitudes. Vertical speeds are usually limited by maximum and minimum vertical speed parameters set by the operator. For rotor-wing aircraft, two meters per second is usually a safe maximum descent rate considering turbulence caused by rotor wash. Rotor-wing aircraft are usually capable of safely achieving higher climb rates than descent rates, but both of these parameters should be verified during flight testing.

/ GPS

A GPS flight mode generally incorporates the same functionality as a Stabilize flight mode, but in addition, it applies dynamic stability to the position of the aircraft determined by the GPS location. This type of mode will usually implement either a position or velocity scheme. A position scheme obeys the logic of an attitude scheme when pitch or roll is commanded but will attempt to maintain GPS position while the RC transmitter stick is in the neutral position. In a velocity scheme, the operator commands the horizontal velocity of the aircraft up to a preset maximum. In this case, when the RC transmitter stick is in the neutral position, a velocity of zero is commanded and the aircraft will attempt to maintain a stationary hover. When the control stick is deflected, the aircraft will attempt to reach the corresponding velocity in the direction of deflection and maintain that speed using GPS.

In both the position scheme and velocity scheme, the operator is not in direct control of the aircraft's attitude, but rather the flight controller will command small attitude deflections in order to maintain GPS position in breezy conditions. Similarly, when the RC transmitter control stick is placed in the neutral position while the aircraft is in motion, the flight controller will usually briefly pitch and/or roll, performing a braking maneuver in order to halt translational motion and maintain GPS position. This reaction is often referred to as braking and may be tuned to provide more aggressive stopping and more accurate positioning, or vice versa.

To recap, let us once again consider the example of a multirotor that receives a brief roll command. The aircraft will either roll to and maintain a specific angle (position scheme, similar to attitude scheme) or dynamically roll to maintain a horizontal speed (velocity scheme). The maximum stick deflection will either correspond to the preset maximum roll angle (position scheme, similar to attitude scheme) or preset maximum velocity (velocity scheme). Once the control stick is returned to neutral in a GPS mode, rather than continuing to move in that direction (as would occur in a Stabilize flight mode), the autopilot will attempt to stop all translational motion and maintain a hover in the position where the control stick was released. This may require a small roll output in the opposite direction. A GPS flight mode provides greater control over the aircraft, preventing drift in windy conditions. In the event of an unexpected condition or emergency requiring manual control, the GPS flight mode will stop motion and put the aircraft in a stable hover until the operator determines how to best respond. A GPS mode using a velocity scheme may also provide more stable and fluid control of a moving aircraft, especially in breezy or turbulent conditions. The downside of GPS modes is that they (obviously) require GPS, which is a system that can fail or, more likely, be adversely affected by interference in the operating environment.

/ GRID

In a Grid mode, the heading of the vehicle is recorded at the time it is armed. This heading becomes the "forward" direction while in Grid mode. Therefore, pushing forward on the pitch stick will move the aircraft in that direction regardless of the direction the nose is pointing. Pulling back on the pitch stick will move the aircraft in the opposite direction. Left and right roll inputs will move the aircraft left and right relative to the recorded "forward" direction. Collective and yaw control will behave normally.

/ RADIUS

In a Radius mode, the GPS position of the vehicle is recorded at the time it is armed. This point now becomes a pivot point about which the aircraft may rotate. Pushing forward on the pitch stick will increase the radius (distance from the point to the aircraft), moving the aircraft directly away from the pivot point. Pulling back on the pitch stick will decrease this radius. Left and right roll inputs will move the aircraft either counterclockwise or clockwise about the pivot point. Collective and yaw control will behave normally. This mode can be useful for flying circular paths around an object on the ground for cinematic footage.

Augmented Fixed-Wing Control Modes

In addition to Stabilize, some flight controllers will provide one of more flight modes intended to better assist the fixed-wing aircraft operator when flying manually. These flight modes may include climb and descent control as well as airspeed control.

/ CLIMB AND DESCENT CONTROL

Flight controllers can attempt to regulate vertical speed (the rate of climb or descent) for augmented manual modes. In fixed-wing aircraft, this is usually controlled via the pitch stick commanding coupled pitch and throttle adjustments. A neutral pitch position will usually command the flight controller to maintain a vertical speed of 0 (level flight). Note that many sensors can factor into the flight controller's calculation of vertical speed including the IMU, barometer, 3D GPS position, and AGL range sensor at low altitudes. Vertical speed is usually limited by maximum and minimum vertical speed parameters set by the operator. Safe climb and descent for fixed-wing aircraft are specific to the airframe and should be determined during flight testing.

/ AIRSPEED CONTROL

Most flight controllers will attempt to regulate the airspeed of a fixed-wing aircraft for augmented manual modes. The airspeed targeted by the flight controller is usually controlled by the throttle stick of the RC transmitter, with the minimum and maximum throttle positions corresponding to preset minimum and maximum airspeed parameters. The setting for the minimum airspeed parameter is intended to avoid a stall, while the maximum airspeed parameter is designed to avoid unnecessary stress on the structure of the aircraft or vibration caused by buffeting. Both of these airspeed parameters should be determined during flight testing. It is important to remember that airspeed (speed through the air as measured by the pitot tube) may differ significantly from ground speed (speed over the ground as determined by the rate of change in GPS position) based on whether the aircraft is travelling into the wind (headwind) or with the wind (tailwind). In a simplified example, if an aircraft is experiencing a headwind, its ground speed will be less than the airspeed, hindered by the headwind. If that aircraft then makes a level, 180-degree turn without changing throttle setting, the airspeed of the aircraft will remain roughly the same but the resulting tailwind will cause the ground speed of the aircraft to increase significantly.

Flight Controller Failsafe

SOME FLIGHT CONTROLLER systems provide for so-called failsafe contingencies designed to prevent an in-flight emergency. These contingencies usually consist of conditions that could lead to an emergency and actions that will be taken in the event of each emergency. Each condition may be specified to invoke a specific action. Failsafe actions are special autonomous flight modes that preempt normal operations. However, in some cases the user may take control of the aircraft back from certain failsafe actions if the failsafe condition is no longer present.

Common Failsafe Conditions

/ BATTERY

In order to prevent the aircraft from inadvertently running out of power, the user may specify a voltage or remaining capacitance measured by the PMU at which a Battery Failsafe condition will be invoked. Some flight controller systems will provide two separate battery conditions: Low Battery Voltage and Critical Battery Voltage.

The Low Battery Voltage condition is meant to be triggered at a level that will allow for several more minutes of flight time, during which the aircraft may return to the home position and land without risking damage to the aircraft or battery. Some flight controllers may offer a smart or dynamic Low Battery Voltage (as opposed to a fixed one), which will attempt to adjust the low voltage trigger value as a function of range from the home position. This feature is intended to trigger the failsafe event with enough battery remaining to return to the home position for landing while maximizing flight time.

The Critical Battery Voltage condition serves as a last chance to prevent damage to the aircraft. At this point, the aircraft will only have enough remaining battery to land at its current position. This may be triggered after the Low Battery Voltage condition when the aircraft has been operating at long range and the remaining battery capacity is not sufficient to return to the home position.

/ GPS

Because flight operations are heavily dependent on GPS signal, the loss of GPS lock can make it unsafe to continue flying autonomously. For this reason, if the strength of the signal received from GPS satellites is significantly degraded, most flight controllers will default to an Attitude mode while others will provide the option to automatically land in place without the ability to maintain position.

/ GEOFENCE

Most mission control software will allow the user to specify a geographic area and altitude range within which the aircraft is safely allowed to operate. The boundary of this region is commonly referred to as a **geofence**. If the aircraft crosses the geofence for any reason, the Geofence condition will trigger.

/ RC LINK LOSS

The RC Link Loss condition is intended to trigger when the received signal strength indication (RSSI) value of the RC receiver measured by the flight controller becomes significantly degraded. This may occur due to range, obstacles, or loss of power of the RC transmitter. The user is usually allowed to enable or disable this feature and set the time delay before the condition is invoked.

/ TELEMETRY LINK LOSS

Similar to the RC Link Loss condition, the Telemetry Link Loss condition will be invoked if the RSSI of the telemetry module is significantly degraded. The user is usually allowed to enable or disable this feature and set the time delay before the condition is invoked.

Actions

Following is a description of each of the failsafe actions: Land Now; Return Home and Land; Return Home, Loiter, and Land; Hold Position; and Report.

/ LAND NOW

In a multicopter, the Land Now action will cause the aircraft to descend for a normal landing at its current location. If the aircraft has lost GPS lock, it will maintain a level attitude while descending; therefore, the aircraft may drift substantially if pushed by the wind. In a fixed-wing, the aircraft will normally execute a gentle descending spiral at a specified radius and landing descent rate until reaching the ground. Land now is often used in the event of Critical Battery Voltage or GPS loss. Note that in the case of GPS loss, there is the potential for wind to blow the aircraft out of position during landing. This displacement can be significant if descending from high altitude.

/ RETURN HOME AND LAND

The Return Home and Land action will cause the aircraft to either climb to a specified altitude or, if already above the specified altitude, maintain its current altitude. This altitude should be high enough to avoid any obstacles in the immediate area. Then the aircraft will transit back to the home position or other specified safe location, where it will execute the Land Now action. Return Home and Land is commonly applied to a low voltage condition, but it could also be used in the case of Link Loss and Geofence breach events based on operator preference.

/ RETURN HOME, LOITER, AND LAND

The Return Home, Loiter, and Land action will cause the aircraft to either climb to a specified altitude or, if already above the specified altitude, maintain its current altitude. This altitude should be high enough to avoid any obstacles in the immediate area. Then the aircraft will transit back to the home position or other specified safe location where it will loiter for a specified duration. This loiter is designed to give the operator time to rectify link issues and reacquire control of the aircraft before landing. Thus, this action can be ideal for Link Loss conditions. After the end of the loiter, the aircraft will execute the Land Now action.

For Return Home, Loiter, and Land, the user-specified values include the return home and land altitude, the loiter duration or end condition, and the home position. This action can be used for most conditions including Geofence and Link Loss conditions.

/ HOLD POSITION (ROTOR WING)

In some cases, it may be desirable for an aircraft to hold position in the event of a failsafe condition. For example, if an aircraft has reached the edge of the geofence, the operator may prefer that the aircraft not RTH. In this case, some flight controllers offer the option to hold position if the operator is providing a command that would violate the geofence, preventing the aircraft from crossing the boundary. Hold Position may also be useful during Link Loss conditions when operating in environments with many obstacles.

/ REPORT

Report is the least invasive action and simply provides the user with an indication, sometimes accompanied by an audible warning, that the condition is occurring. This action is not recommended for most cases.

Failsafe Summary

Table 3-1 shows failsafe conditions and the recommended actions to invoke should they occur. It is important to note that in many cases, there is no substitute for a competent pilot capable of safely landing the aircraft.

Table 3-1. Common Conditions and Recommended Failsafe Actions

CONDITION	RECOMMENDED ACTION	CONDITION	RECOMMENDED ACTION
Low Battery Voltage	Return Home and Land	Geofence	Return Home, Loiter and Land
Critical Battery Voltage	Land Now	RC Link Loss	Return Home, Loiter and Land
GPS	Land Now	Telemetry Link Loss	Return Home, Loiter and Land

CHAPTER FOUR

Regulations

As of the time of publishing, the operation of small civilian unmanned aircraft may be divided into two categories: recreational (hobby) and commercial.

Recreational Use

THE RECREATIONAL USE of unmanned aircraft is governed by the same regulations that allow for RC aircraft flight: Section 336 of Public Law 112-95. The Federal Aviation Administration (FAA) summarizes these rules as follows[1]:

1. Fly at or below 400 feet.
2. Keep your UAS within sight.
3. Never fly near other aircraft, especially near airports.
4. Never fly over groups of people.
5. Never fly over stadiums or sports events.
6. Never fly near emergency response efforts such as fires.
7. Never fly under the influence.
8. Be aware of airspace requirements.

These guidelines establish several definitive limitations on recreational aircraft (mainly altitude, weight, line-of-sight, and distance from airports), but also several subjective limitations. Unfortunately, several unmanned aircraft operators have chosen to be rather liberal with their interpretations of terms such as "well clear" and "careless or reckless" and ended up on the evening news for endangering a commercial aircraft. Unfortunately, common sense has become less common and the FAA is cracking down more and more on the resulting violations.

Below its surface, the second rule (keep the aircraft within visual line-of-sight at all times) does rely on a pilot's judgement. The ability to successfully intervene in the event of an unexpected maneuver or action drops off significantly with increasing range as it becomes much more difficult to determine the heading and attitude of the aircraft. Therefore, the **visual line-of-sight (VLOS)** range must be determined not only by the ability to see the aircraft but also by the ability to control the aircraft. As a general rule, the distance at which a pilot can successfully determine the heading and orientation of the aircraft is usually no more than 750 meters slant range (meaning straight line distance from the observer's eye to the aircraft). This is, of course, dependent on the size and markings of the aircraft as well as environmental conditions such as cloud cover and lighting. The VLOS distance should be considered for flight planning, as either this range or the effective range of the video transmitter system is

---

[1] Federal Aviation Administration, *Fly for Fun* webpage, https://www.faa.gov/uas/model_aircraft

usually the limiting factor in determining the aircraft's effective mission area. The FAA specifies that the VLOS range must not depend on the use of aides such as binoculars. VLOS obviously would be broken by flying behind obstacles such as structures, vegetation and terrain, so these should be taken into consideration during preflight planning and when selecting the mission altitude and observation position(s). The VLOS requirement not only promotes safety but also serves to protect your investment in an aircraft.

All small unmanned aircraft (defined as weighing 0.55–55 pounds), including those used for recreation, must be registered with the FAA as described in the Small UAS Registration section of this chapter and in 14 CFR Part 48. Heavier aircraft fall under another category and must follow separate, more stringent regulations.

Commercial Use

THE FAA'S SMALL UNMANNED AIRCRAFT regulations contained in 14 CFR Part 107 establish provisions for a Remote Pilot Certificate (RPC), a means of certifying operators of small unmanned aircraft. In order to be issued an RPC, a person must:

- Be at least 16 years old
- Be able to read, speak, write, and understand English (exceptions may be made if the person is unable to meet one of these requirements for a medical reason, such as hearing impairment)
- Be in a physical and mental condition to safely operate a small UAS
- Pass the initial aeronautical knowledge exam at an FAA-approved knowledge testing center

Individuals who already hold a Part 61 pilot certificate other than that of a student pilot (for manned aviation) may follow an abbreviated process, leveraging the aviation knowledge they already have, to receive an RPC. Consult a flight instructor or the FAA website for more details on this process.

The FAA has provided study material for preparing for the Remote Pilot Certificate airman knowledge test, as well as information regarding the test itself and appropriate testing centers. You can access many of these online by visiting www.asa2fly.com/reader/tpuas. These resources include:

- FAA Remote Pilot—*Small Unmanned Aircraft Systems Airman Certification Standards* (FAA-S-ACS-10).
- FAA Remote Pilot—*Small Unmanned Aircraft Systems Study Guide* (FAA-G-8082-22)
- FAA Advisory Circular 107-2, *Small Unmanned Aircraft Systems* (sUAS)

- FAA's Unmanned Aircraft Systems webpage (www.faa.gov/uas), which provides additional aeronautical knowledge resources, test sample questions, and test instructions.
- FAA *Pilot's Handbook of Aeronautical Knowledge* (FAA-H-8083-25)

The Remote Pilot Certificate with an sUAS Rating airman knowledge test prepares pilots to safely operate their aircraft by informing them of the regulations, which include adherence to the guidelines discussed under the Recreational Use section of this chapter, but with several notable additions:

- Pilots manipulating the controls of a small UAS aircraft must possess or be under the direct supervision of a crew member who possesses a valid RPC as described above. The holder of the RPC must be able and prepared to take control of the aircraft if safety dictates. This crew member must also have the certificate on their person when intending to operate.
- Operators who are flying using FPV or live video systems that divert their attention from observing the aircraft must be assisted by a **visual observer (VO)**, a crew member tasked with observing the aircraft at all times. The pilot and visual observer must maintain communications throughout all flight operations. Visual observers must also obey the unaided VLOS requirement. Visual observers should also be used to assist pilots when another perspective of the aircraft would increase the safety of operations, such as when operating in close proximity to structures. While required for safety in some cases, visual observers are not required to hold an RPC.
- The takeoff weight of the aircraft—including any removable components such as batteries, operational payload (e.g., sensors), and cargo payload—may not exceed 55 pounds during any phase of the operation.
- No pilot or visual observer may be responsible for more than one aircraft at a time.
- Aircraft may be operated during daylight hours. An aircraft may also be operated during twilight if it is equipped with appropriate anti-collision lighting. Twilight hours are defined as the two separate 30-minute periods immediately prior to official sunset and immediately after official sunrise. All other times are considered night hours, during which operations are prohibited.
- Visibility must be no less than 3 statute miles from the control station.
- The aircraft must be operated no less than 500 feet below clouds and no less than 2,000 feet horizontally from clouds.
- Aircraft may not operate more than 400 feet above ground level (AGL). However, an aircraft may exceed this limitation when operating within a 400-foot radius of a structure, but must not fly higher than 400 feet

above the structure's highest point. This exception is intended to allow for small UAS to conduct structural inspections.

- No aircraft may exceed 100 mph or 87 knots.

- Aircraft may not operate over people unless the people are participating in the operation, under a covered structure, or inside of a covered vehicle.

- Aircraft may not be operated from a moving land or water-borne vehicle except in a sparsely populated area. (Operation from a moving aircraft is prohibited.) The term "sparsely populated" has always been loosely defined by the FAA and often relies on pilot discretion.

- Aircraft are allowed to operate in Class G airspace without prior approval as long as all other regulations are followed. Operations in Class B, C, D, or E airspace require prior approval from the appropriate Air Traffic Control (ATC) authority responsible for that airspace. ATC may require additional equipment (e.g., transponder) on the aircraft and/or may dictate procedures for the operation, such as requiring that radio contact be maintained between the UAS operation and air traffic controllers. It is the responsibility of the operator to determine what airspace they intend to operate in prior to takeoff, remain clear of airspace which they are not authorized to enter, and request permission to enter airspace when appropriate. Airspace classes are described in Chapter 15 of the FAA's *Pilot's Handbook of Aeronautical Knowledge* (www.faa.gov/regulations_policies/handbooks_manuals/aviation/phak).

- Aircraft may carry external loads as long as these loads do not adversely affect flight characteristics and they are securely attached to the aircraft to prevent them from inadvertently detaching during flight. The 55 pound weight limitation must also include these loads.

- Aircraft may carry loads for compensation or hire within state boundaries as long as the 55 pound weight limitation is obeyed at all times during operations.

- Small unmanned aircraft must be registered with the FAA and marked appropriately as described in the Small UAS Registration section of this chapter and in 14 CFR Part 48.

- The pilot must conduct an operational check prior to flight, referred to as a preflight check. The FAA does not dictate specific airworthiness standards as with manned aircraft, and preflight inspections will vary based on the aircraft and payload. However, pilots are required to develop and follow a preflight procedure based on their judgement and including but not limited to manufacturer-recommended procedures for their aircraft and systems (if available). The FAA does specifically reference verifying the link between the ground station and the aircraft as an example of a preflight check. Chapter 6 of this book may be useful for operators as they develop preflight procedures.

- The aircraft and any associated records must be made available to the FAA upon request.
- Any incident that results in serious injury, loss of consciousness, and/or damage to property (other than the aircraft) totaling $500 or more must be reported to the FAA within 10 days.
- Waivers may be granted for most regulations if it can be shown that the proposed operation may be conducted safely. These waivers may be requested through the FAA's online portal at www.faa.gov/uas/request_waiver.

Small UAS Registration

14 CFR PART 107 also establishes provisions for a Federal Drone Registration; these registration requirements are further clarified in 14 CFR Part 48. Operators of unmanned aircraft weighing between 0.55 and 55 pounds—whether used for recreational or commercial purposes, and even those without flight controllers (which may be otherwise defined as RC aircraft)—must apply for registration online through the FAA website. Note that the weight limitation refers to the takeoff weight of the aircraft including any removable components such as batteries and payload. Aircraft weighing less than 0.55 pounds require no registration, while those that weigh more than 55 pounds follow separate registration guidelines. The registration process is fairly simple and requires that the operator:

- Be 13 years of age or older. (If the owner is less than 13 years of age, a person 13 years of age or older must register the small unmanned aircraft.)
- Be a U.S. citizen or legal permanent resident.
- Provide an email address.
- Pay the $5 fee with a credit or debit card.
- Provide a physical address and mailing address (if different from physical address).

When registering an aircraft for commercial use, more specific information—such as make, model, and serial number for the specific aircraft being registered—must be provided. Once the application is completed, operators will receive an email from the FAA with a registration certificate, which is valid for 3 years and must be in the operator's possession when intending to fly. The certificate also contains a registration number, which must be affixed to the aircraft in such a way that it will remain affixed, is clearly legible, and may be accessed without tools. Hobbyists (who use their aircraft purely for recreation) will be issued a single registration number for all of the aircraft they own, while each aircraft used for commercial purposes must have a unique registration number.

The Academy of Model Aeronautics (AMA)

THE ACADEMY OF MODEL AERONAUTICS (AMA) is the national body for remote control flying as well as other forms of model aviation in the United States. Membership in the AMA can provide two valuable benefits to small UAS operators:

1. Liability, medical, fire, and theft insurance as long as the operator is in good standing within the AMA and following the AMA's National Model Aircraft Safety Code, which in most cases echoes the regulations of Part 107. (See www.modelaircraft.org/files/105.pdf)

2. Access to AMA-approved flying sites across the United States. These fields can serve as a safe and acceptable place to learn to fly and to practice commercial operation techniques. However, note that many of these sites are operated and maintained by private RC flying clubs that may require membership dues in addition to AMA membership.

In addition, the AMA prides itself on standing up for the rights of recreational RC pilots to practice their hobby safely and respectfully. These interests are often mutual to both traditional RC pilots and small UAS operators.

The advent of small unmanned aircraft technology has been something of a mixed blessing for the AMA. On the one hand, this technology has revitalized interest in small-scale, unmanned aviation as a hobby, which had been suffering in previous years. But with the FAA stepping in to regulate these aircraft, the AMA has struggled a bit to establish its identity moving forward. Furthermore, a divide sometimes exists between old-school RC pilots—who have been flying for years without the aid of flight controllers and FPV systems—and new small UAS operators who have embraced this new technology and are arguably the future of the hobby but who do not necessarily value the same skills as their predecessors. Even so, many traditional RC pilots are very welcoming to new members as long as they follow the rules of safety and flying etiquette (which is good for everyone), and RC pilots can also be a great source of knowledge about flying. In this way, the AMA provides a community that fosters development and safety of both RC and UAS flying. While it is not required by Part 107, membership in the AMA, as well as adherence to the AMA's Safety Code, is highly recommended for both recreational and commercial UAS operators.

CHAPTER FIVE

Flight Testing Process

Flight testing is essential if you are building your own custom aircraft, but it can also be a great way to familiarize yourself with and validate an off-the-shelf aircraft. Flight testing is also necessary after significantly changing the configuration of an aircraft—for example, after adding a new payload. This flight testing process should include but not be limited to the following considerations and steps.

Multicopter Flight Testing

Selecting a Suitable Test Site

Dry soccer fields, especially with artificial turf, may be ideal for use as test sites. For safety reasons, avoid flying near people and obstacles during the flight testing process. Also attempt to conduct flight testing in still air. Early mornings can be suitable for both.

Safety

Begin by conducting a thorough preflight check with special emphasis on construction, GPS/compass performance, and RC response. Then move to and maintain a safe distance; 10 meters from the aircraft is usually acceptable. Also remember to place the aircraft with its front or nose pointed away from you for takeoffs during flight testing. This will make the aircraft easier to control in the event that you must intervene quickly. It is also a good idea to configure a kill switch on the RC transmitter to allow the aircraft's motors to be stopped in an emergency. This will cause the aircraft to fall and will likely result in significant damage, but may prevent a fly-away or personal injury.

Arming and Tip Over/Control Checks

By this point, motor set up, calibration, and bench testing should be completed, verifying that the flight controller, ESCs, and motors have been correctly configured and reducing the likelihood that the aircraft will become uncontrollable. The ultimate test, however, is an arming and tip over check.

Begin by arming the aircraft in a stabilized flight mode and observe that all propellers spin up to idle without any indication that the aircraft is becoming unstable on the ground. If the aircraft has been configured incorrectly, it will likely begin to tip over at this point. If the aircraft appears stable, it may be possible to check pitch and roll controls without fully lifting off the ground. If these channels have been incorrectly assigned or reversed, the consequences will be much more severe after the aircraft is in the air. Apply small to medium pitch and roll changes and observe the airframe tilt slightly in the expected direction. If you observe an unexpected result, then disarm the aircraft and attempt to correct the problem by checking the assignment and direction of these channels. In any case, be prepared to throttle down or kill power if the aircraft appears to be tipping over.

Low Hover Check

The aircraft may now be considered safe for takeoff. Gradually increase the throttle until the aircraft lifts off the ground, then immediately begin a low hover control check. Bring the aircraft into a hover about one meter above the ground. This height will reduce damage if testing is unsuccessful. If the aircraft wobbles severely in a hover, land and verify that all ESCs are properly set up and calibrated. If so, this instability may be an indication that the gains are set too high. Next, make small attitude inputs in pitch and roll; this will allow you to maintain a stationary hover, but more importantly it will allow you to verify that the pitch and roll channels have been properly assigned. If these inputs produce an unexpected aircraft maneuver, be prepared to immediately cut the throttle or kill the power as the aircraft will be nearly impossible to control if a control axis is reversed or improperly assigned. If the aircraft appears to be maneuvering correctly and stable, apply small, instantaneous (step inputs) pitch and roll inputs and observe the aircraft as it returns to a level condition. This will allow you to familiarize yourself with how the aircraft handles and may provide indications about how the aircraft should be tuned.

Hover Throttle Setting with Dummy Payload Weight

In this next step, attempt to maintain a level, stationary hover for several minutes. Some flight controllers will "learn" the correct motor output for a level hover over time. Others may require this setting to be manually input after being determined from motor output levels when held in a hover (determined from flight logs). Ideally, the aircraft will hover at around the mid-throttle setting (50% power), but underpowered or overloaded aircraft may require more power. This setting should be gathered with an attached dummy weight to represent the payload. A small sand bag or water bottle may work well.

Pitch and Roll PID Tuning with Dummy Payload Weight

Once the hover throttle setting has been applied (which may require landing and inspecting the flight log), the aircraft may begin PID tuning with a dummy payload weight. (For a more detailed description of PID loops and tuning, please see the end of this chapter.) Begin by climbing the aircraft to a safe altitude; 3–5 meters usually works well. Then begin tuning the aircraft by issuing small and then larger step inputs in pitch and roll and observing the aircraft's response in a stabilized flight mode. Increasing the P term (Proportional) will cause the aircraft to return more quickly to a level orientation. Increasing the D term (Differential) may be used to limit overshoot as the aircraft returns to level. Finally, increasing the I term (Integral) may be used to dampen out vibrations over time. Manually tuning may be accomplished first by visually observing the aircraft and next by observing attitude offset charts, which is allowed by most flight controllers through the GCS software.

Some flight controllers will also allow for an automatic tuning mode, which may be assigned to a switch on the RC transmitter for flight testing. In the auto tune flight mode, the flight controller will issue pitch and roll step inputs while iteratively adjusting the appropriate gains until arriving at suitable values. This process is repeatable and has proven to be very effective for small multicopters, but it is important to provide the aircraft with enough space to fully execute the auto tuning process. It is also important to be vigilant and prepared to take manual control if any malfunction is observed.

Yaw Testing with Dummy Payload Weight

Yaw testing may be used to verify the flight controller configuration as well as the mechanical assembly of the aircraft. Provide the aircraft with small and then larger yaw step inputs in both directions and observe the response. If the yaw appears to be "sloppy"—overshooting the heading in one direction while undershooting in the other—this may be an indication that one or more motor mounts is not level, skewing thrust in one direction. This should be corrected before any yaw PID tuning is applied, if necessary. Meanwhile, if you notice a drift in heading, the inability of the aircraft to hold its position in a neutral hover, or the aircraft exhibiting a sloppy spiraling maneuver, these may be indications that the compass calibration is inadequate. If yaw tuning and compass calibration is satisfactory, the aircraft may be placed in a GPS hold mode and yawed in a complete 360-degree turn. If GPS hold is functioning correctly, the aircraft should maintain position within a satisfactory margin regardless of heading. This maneuver may produce small fluctuations in altitude; these fluctuations are normal but may be addressed through altitude hold tuning, if desired.

Altitude Hold Tuning with Dummy Payload Weight

Once the aircraft's maneuvering controls have been properly tuned and verified, the ability of the flight controller to hold altitude should be tested. First, place the aircraft in a stabilized flight mode, then apply up and down step inputs and observe the aircraft's response. Tune the altitude hold PID values as necessary to reduce over-shoot and oscillations in the vertical axis. Next, place the aircraft in an altitude hold flight mode (if available) and fly the aircraft in a small box pattern. During maneuvers, the aircraft should hold altitude within an acceptable tolerance. Small fluctuations in altitude while the aircraft is in motion may be the result of pressure fluctuations around the flight controller's barometer.

Maximum Horizontal Speed Setting

Flying in a box or rectangular pattern also provides an opportunity to set the maximum lateral speed of the aircraft. This maximum should be set at a speed at which the aircraft does not feel unsafe or unstable. If the aircraft seems to be trans-lating slightly sideways, the compass calibration may be inadequate.

Climb Rate Settings

Next, set the climb and descent rate of the aircraft to appropriate values. The climb rate limit should be high enough to allow for an expedient climb but low enough that a full climb does not result in an excessive drop in battery voltage, potentially triggering a Low Battery Voltage failsafe condition. Descent rates should allow for an expedient descent but not result in an unsafe speed toward the ground or excessive buffeting due to descent through rotor wash. Once climb and descent rates have been properly tuned, they should be tested in an Altitude Hold mode.

Autonomous Test with Dummy Payload Weight

At this point, the aircraft is safe to attempt an autonomous flight plan. First, make sure the geofence and failsafe settings are appropriate for the environment, flight plan, aircraft, and battery. The aircraft is then ready to execute an autonomous takeoff and be sent into a looping box pattern (e.g., completing waypoint 4 sends the aircraft back to waypoint 1) at an altitude of about 10 meters. First, create this flight plan with constant altitude and ground speed. Observe the aircraft as it maneuvers; ideally, it will be able to maintain these parameters without excessive oscillations. Next, intro-duce climbs and descents as well as changes in airspeed. As the aircraft loops through the flight plan, carefully make small adjustments to gains on the fly through the GCS software and observe whether the change produces the desired effect. For safety, make only one minor change at a time and double-check new values before sending them to the aircraft. This is also an opportunity to observe the aircraft's heading behavior as it flies on the legs of the flight plan. Some flight controllers allow the user to specify the aircraft's heading behavior when it reaches a waypoint, either maintaining constant heading or yawing to face the next waypoint, similar to a manned aircraft. Finally, an autonomous landing should be tested, observing the aircraft descent rate and the ground detection feature. Be prepared to take manual control or kill the aircraft in the event of an unintended or unsafe maneuver.

Failsafe Test with Dummy Payload Weight

Testing failsafe conditions is essential for safe operations, but these tests should not be taken lightly, as they involve placing the aircraft in a potentially unsafe condition. It is also important for an operator to understand proper failsafe procedures. Before any such testing, thoroughly check the failsafe settings, including minimum safe voltage, maximum altitude, and geofence placement, as well as specified actions in the event of conditions such as RC Link Loss, Telemetry Link Loss, Geofence breach, Low Battery Voltage, Critical Battery Voltage, and Return to Home. It is important to remember that, because these failsafe conditions often require an autonomous landing and may involve loss of control link, the aircraft must be preprogrammed for landing configuration in that a failsafe action triggers. The most common example is programming the landing gear to lower automatically in the event of failsafe.

/ RETURN TO HOME

Return to Home (RTH) is a special flight mode that may be invoked when a failsafe condition is reached, but it can also be useful when configured to a switch on the RC transmitter. In RTH mode, the aircraft will either climb to a specified altitude or maintain a constant altitude (if already above the RTH altitude). The RTH altitude is intended to place the aircraft above any obstacles in the immediate area and should be altered prior to each flight to maintain safety. After reaching the appropriate altitude, the flight controller will maneuver the aircraft directly back to its home position, which is normally where the aircraft was first armed, but this position may be edited in flight. Upon reaching the home point, the aircraft will begin a vertical descent until landing. In the event of an emergency, this flight mode can be invoked using a specially configured switch in order to bring the aircraft back to its starting point. Such a switch should also be used to test RTH during autonomous flight testing.

/ VOLTAGE FAILSAFE

Once the RTH mode has been tested, the next step is testing the failsafe conditions, as these procedures will depend on RTH. Almost all flight controllers allow users to specify a low voltage level that when reached will automatically trigger failsafe and the RTH flight mode in order to prevent the aircraft from running out of battery in flight. This voltage should allow adequate flight time for the aircraft to execute the RTH action without potentially damaging the battery (3.5–3.6 volts per LiPo cell is usually adequate). Some flight controllers also allow the user to specify a critical voltage at which the aircraft will land at its current location, serving as a last resort to prevent battery damage and a potential crash. The voltage failsafe may be tested by flying the aircraft until the specified low voltage setting is reached. However, extreme caution should be observed because in the event of an unintended maneuver, minimal flight time remains to safely correct. Only execute the voltage failsafe while having a clear view of the aircraft and in a position to take control and land immediately if necessary.

/ GEOFENCE FAILSAFE

The simplest form of geofence is defined by a maximum altitude or ceiling and radius from the home position, but it may also be defined by a user-drawn polygon. These parameters create an enclosure that, if breached by the aircraft, will invoke failsafe and execute either an immediate landing or an RTH action. In most circumstances, RTH is recommended, as it reduces the likelihood of landing in an unsafe area and allows the operator the opportunity to retake control (by toggling the flight mode selector on the RC transmitter). Both the altitude and lateral limits of the geofence should be verified during geofence testing by attempting to fly the aircraft out of the geofence area both vertically and horizontally while at all times being ready to retake control if necessary.

/ RC LINK LOSS

If the flight controller detects that it is no longer receiving input from the RC receiver, it may be configured to invoke failsafe and either land immediately or execute RTH (which should be predetermined by the user based on the operating environment). This feature is designed to prevent the aircraft from continuing flight out of RC range. Some RC receiver systems are equipped with their own failsafe system, which is intended to allow an RC pilot to specify outputs from the receiver in the event that link is lost. However, if used in conjunction with an autonomous system, the RC system failsafe should be disabled or configured such that it invokes the flight controller failsafes. Some flight controllers will allow an operator to disable the RC Link Loss failsafe when the aircraft is in an autonomous flight mode. This prevents autonomous flight from being interrupted while the flight controller is flying the aircraft. However, this eliminates one means of intervening in the event of an unintended maneuver.

The RC Link Loss failsafe should be tested by turning off the RC transmitter while in flight. This test should be performed using extreme caution, preferably with a second operator controlling the GCS and able to intervene quickly if necessary. In order to reestablish control through the RC transmitter, the operator must first turn it back on and then toggle the flight mode selector.

/ TELEMETRY LINK LOSS

Some flight controllers will allow for the triggering of failsafe in the event that link is lost with the GCS through the telemetry module. This event will be triggered after a given period of time (ten seconds is usually adequate) and will result in either an immediate landing or the RTH action as predetermined by the user based on the operating environment. Like the RC Link Loss feature, some flight controllers will allow the user to specify whether Telemetry Link Loss during manual flight (control through the RC transmitter) will invoke failsafe. Telemetry Link Loss should be tested during autonomous flight by disconnecting the ground telemetry module from the GCS laptop or tablet and waiting for the link loss to take effect. An operator should be ready to take over with the RC transmitter in the event of an unintended maneuver.

Mode Checks with Dummy Payload Weight

Any flight modes applicable to normal operations of the vehicle should be tested at this time, ensuring that they are properly configured on the aircraft and on the RC transmitter. This is also an opportunity for operators to ensure they are comfortable with the maneuvers produced by these flight modes as well as the transitions between modes. At this point, any controls configured on the RC transmitter that are specific to flight testing—such as auto tune, manually tuning, and, based on pilot's preference, kill—are removed prior to normal operations.

Flight Test with Live Payload

Testing with a live payload may now begin. First, however, it may be necessary to perform a magnetometer calibration and/or RC range check due to the installation of metal or carbon structures that are part of the payload. Flight testing with a live payload may be used to verify that the aircraft maneuvers correctly with the gain values arrived at during flight testing, as well as to verify correct gimbal function and video transmitter range in various aircraft orientations.

Fixed-Wing Aircraft Flight Testing

FIXED-WING FLIGHT testing requires much more RC experience and finesse than multicopter flight testing. The following sections outline what fixed-wing flight testing conducted by a capable RC pilot will include.

Selecting a Suitable Test Site

When selecting a suitable test site, remember that fixed-wing aircraft require large operating areas free of obstacles and flat, smooth landing zones with clear approach paths. Consider joining the Academy of Model Aeronautics (AMA) to gain access to approved RC flying sites. For safety reasons, try to avoid flying near people during the flight testing process. Also attempt to conduct flight testing in still air. Early mornings can be suitable for meeting both of these requirements.

Safety

Begin by familiarizing yourself with the operating area, including areas to avoid in the event of an emergency, such as areas occupied by people and bodies of water. Then, conduct a thorough preflight check with special emphasis on construction, GPS/compass performance, airspeed sensor calibration, and RC response.

RC Flight Check with Dummy Payload

While flying either in RC Mode or with the MUX engaged, complete the following steps or checks (covered in detail below): run-up, takeoff, aircraft trim/throws, cruising speed, stall speed, climb rate, maximum safe airspeed, descent rate, and landing approach. Airspeeds can be read from the flight control software. It is important to simulate the weight and configuration of the payload during these tests, achieving the weight balance of the aircraft during actual mission conditions and allowing accurate tuning. The following tests may be achieved either using a MUX or prior to flight controller installation.

/ RUN-UP

It is important to conduct an initial run-up of the motor on the ground. With the aircraft safely held or otherwise secured, gradually increase the throttle to 100%. Bear in mind that it can be dangerous to hold this throttle setting for too long, especially without airflow over the motor and ESC. This is an opportunity to verify that the motor and propeller are properly secured, the thrust output is sufficient, and vibrations do not seem excessive.

/ TAKEOFF

An initial takeoff test should be conducted with the throttle set to 100%. All takeoff tests should be conducted in a direction that will allow for an abort landing to be conducted safely, if necessary. Once you establish that the aircraft can safely take off with full throttle, lower throttle settings may be tested, but likely not less than 75%. This throttle setting should lend itself to a climb rate that allows the aircraft to quickly reach a safe altitude. This climb rate may be greater than the normal mission climb rate described later. The throttle setting and takeoff climb rate should be recorded for later programming into the flight controller.

/ AIRCRAFT TRIM AND THROWS

In straight-and-level flight, first verify that the aircraft is properly trimmed. As long as the aircraft is reasonably symmetrical and balanced, it should only require pitch trimming in order to maintain level flight. For example, if constant back pressure on the trim stick is required, adjust the trim tab downward until this pressure is no longer necessary. It should be noted that the deployment flaps will likely result in a pitch-up tendency, requiring more nose down trim, which can be achieved in the flight controller through channel mixing.

Next, execute progressively larger pitch and roll maneuvers in order to test the throws of the ailerons. An unmanned aircraft should be reasonably responsive but not excessively maneuverable. The travel or end points of a particular channel may be adjusted in order to achieve the desired maneuverability.

After landing, these values should be transferred to the flight controller and also set to sub-trims. This is best done by measuring the physical distance between the neutral position and maximum throw of each surface and adjusting flight controller settings until these same measurements are reached. The same should be done for the sub-trims of the RC transmitter, allowing the trims to be set back to zero. Finally, if a MUX is used, verify that switching between the MUX and the flight controller does not result in motion of the control surfaces, both while the sticks are at neutral and at their limits.

/ CRUISING SPEED

In level flight, establish a speed that seems natural for the aircraft—fast enough that it is not at risk of a stall but slow enough that it is able to maneuver, turn effectively, and is not subject to vibrations that can be induced at high speeds. Ideally, in still air, this speed should be achieved at or near the mid-throttle setting. Otherwise, the aircraft may be overpowered or underpowered. This cruising speed should be recorded for later programming into the flight controller.

/ STALL SPEED

While cruising at a safe, high altitude (no less than 40 meters over a safe area), stall the aircraft by cutting the throttle and applying pitch-up pressure. The speed at which the aircraft stalls should be used as a reference for the minimum safe airspeed during autonomous flight. Also note the behavior of the aircraft before and after the stall. Ideally, an aircraft will "break cleanly," dipping its nose straight downward. Unstable aircraft are at risk of entering a spin after a stall, which can be very difficult for flight controllers to recover from.

In order to recover from a stall or near stall in an RC mode:

1. Neutralize ailerons.
2. Pitch nose downward to break stall and regain airspeed.
3. Smoothly increase throttle and reestablish positive climb.

To recover from a spin in an RC mode:

1. Cut throttle.
2. Neutralize ailerons.

3. Pitch nose downward to break stall and regain airspeed.

4. Apply rudder in the opposite direction of the spin.

5. Smoothly increase throttle and reestablish positive climb.

Note that the deployment of flaps can significantly change the stall characteristics of an aircraft and also reduce its stall speed.

/ CLIMB RATE

Climb rate testing may be performed after takeoff when the aircraft has established a safe maneuvering altitude (40 meters is adequate in most cases) and a positive rate of climb. With the throttle set to achieve the normal cruising speed determined earlier, establish a climb rate that seems natural for the aircraft, neither sluggish nor exhibiting signs of nearing stall. This climb rate should be recorded for later programming into the flight controller.

/ MAXIMUM SAFE AIRSPEED

While maintaining a straight heading and level altitude, gradually increase the throttle and observe the effects on the aircraft. Determine a maximum safe airspeed that will not produce excessive fluttering of the wings or tail, which is a source of vibration and structural stress. An onboard camera installed for flight testing can be useful for monitoring structural vibrations. Record this airspeed for later programming into the flight controller.

/ DESCENT RATE

With the throttle set to achieve the normal cruising speed determined earlier, pitch down to achieve a natural descent rate that allows for a brisk descent but does not exceed the maximum safe airspeed. Record this value for later programming into the flight controller.

/ LANDING APPROACH

Attempt several landing approaches in order to determine an ideal landing approach speed and descent rate. The approach speed will likely be approximately 1.25 times the stall speed, and the descent rate will be less than or equal to the normal mission descent rate determined above.

Configuring the Flight Controller

Enter the values determined in the RC flight checks into the flight controller along with the minimum safe altitude, pitch and roll limits (±10 degrees for pitch and ±30 degrees for roll are suitable for most aircraft), and geofence parameter.

Stabilized Flight Check with Dummy Payload

Begin a stabilized flight check by performing a manual takeoff and then switching into a stabilized mode from straight-and-level flight. Observe that the aircraft transfers smoothly to flight controller authority. Next, disturb the aircraft from level flight, attempting climbs, descents, rolls, and throttle changes with momentary step inputs, observe the response, and tune as necessary. Verify the limits previously programmed in the flight controller by performing the following checks:

- Verify the attitude limits by applying maximum stick inputs in pitch and roll.
- Verify the maximum and minimum airspeeds by setting the throttle to both its maximum and minimum positions for several seconds.
- Verify the climb and descent rate settings by establishing sustained climb and descents for several seconds.
- Verify the aircraft ability to maintain altitude by releasing it to level flight after both climbing and descending. Tune the governing altitude hold parameters as necessary.

Autonomous Flight Check with Dummy Payload

From a stabilized flight mode, launch the aircraft into an autonomous mission. A looping box pattern with climbs, descents, and airspeed changes works well to apply changes to the parameters governing autonomous flight and observe the effects. Consider adjusting airspeed governing, altitude governing, autonomous path tracking, and waypoint radius parameters.

Autonomous Launch and Landing with Dummy Payload

While prepared to take manual or stabilized control, attempt several iterations of auto launch and landing, adjusting parameters as necessary. For more specific details, consult the section in Chapter 3 that covers these flight modes.

Failsafe Checks with Dummy Payload

Testing failsafe conditions is essential for safe operations. These tests should not be taken lightly, as they involve placing the aircraft in a potentially unsafe condition. It is important that operators understand proper failsafe procedures. Before any such testing, thoroughly check the failsafe settings, including minimum safe voltage, maximum altitude, and geofence placement, as well as specified actions in the event of

RC Link Loss, Telemetry Link Loss, Geofence breach, Low Battery Voltage, Critical Battery Voltage, and Return to Home. It is important to remember that, because these failsafe checks often require an autonomous landing and might involve loss of control link, the aircraft must be preprogrammed for the landing configuration in the event that a failsafe action triggers. The most common example is programming the landing gear to lower automatically in the event of failsafe.

/ RETURN TO HOME

Return to Home (RTH) can be considered a special flight mode that may be invoked when a failsafe condition is reached, but it can also be useful when assigned to a switch on the RC transmitter. In RTH mode, most fixed-wing aircraft will either climb to a specified altitude or maintain a constant altitude (if already above the RTH altitude). The RTH altitude is intended to place the aircraft above any obstacles in the immediate area and should be altered prior to each flight to maintain safety. After reaching the appropriate altitude, the flight controller will normally maneuver the aircraft directly back to its home position or other user-specified loiter position. Upon reaching the specified position, the aircraft will begin a loiter at a specified altitude. Most aircraft can be programmed to execute a spiral landing immediately, wait for a specific period of time, or wait until a Low Battery Voltage failsafe occurs. A specially configured switch may be used to invoke this flight mode in the event of an emergency to bring the aircraft back to its starting point. Such a switch should also be used to test RTH during autonomous flight testing.

/ VOLTAGE FAILSAFE

Once the RTH mode has been tested, you may move on to testing the failsafe conditions, as these procedures will depend on RTH. As previously mentioned, almost all flight controllers allow users to specify a low voltage level that, when reached, will trigger failsafe and the RTH flight mode in order to prevent the aircraft from running out of battery in flight. This voltage should allow adequate flight time for the aircraft to execute the RTH action without potentially damaging the battery (3.5–3.6 volts per LiPo cell is usually adequate). Some flight controllers also allow the user to specify a critical battery voltage, which, if reached, will invoke a Land Now action, usually entering a descending spiral at a specified radius and the landing descent rate.

The voltage failsafe may be tested by flying the aircraft until the specified low voltage setting is reached. However, extreme caution should be observed because in the event of an unintended maneuver, little flight time remains to safely correct. Only execute the voltage failsafe while having a clear view of the aircraft and in a position to take control and land immediately if necessary.

/ GEOFENCE FAILSAFE

As previously described, the simplest form of geofence is defined by a maximum altitude or ceiling and radius from the home position, but it may also be defined by a user-drawn polygon. These parameters create an enclosure that, if breached by the aircraft, will invoke failsafe and either execute an immediate landing or an RTH action. In most circumstances, RTH is recommended, reducing the likelihood of a landing in an unsafe area and allowing the operator the opportunity to retake control (by toggling the flight mode selector on the RC transmitter). Both the altitude and lateral limits of the geofence should be verified during geofence testing by attempting to fly the aircraft out of the geofence area both vertically and horizontally while at all times being ready to retake control if necessary.

/ RC LINK LOSS

If the flight controller detects that it is no longer receiving input from the RC receiver, it may be configured to invoke failsafe and either land immediately or execute RTH (a choice predetermined by the user based on the operating environment). This feature is designed to prevent the aircraft from continuing flight out of RC range. Some RC receiver systems are equipped with their own failsafe system, which is intended to allow an RC pilot to specify outputs from the receiver in the event that link is lost. However, if used in conjunction with an autonomous system, the RC system failsafe should be disabled or configured so that the flight controller failsafe is invoked. Some flight controllers will allow an operator to disable the RC Link Loss failsafe when the aircraft is in an autonomous flight mode. This prevents autonomous flight from being interrupted while the flight controller is flying the aircraft. However, this eliminates one means of intervening in the event of an unintended maneuver.

The RC Link Loss failsafe should be tested by turning off the RC transmitter while in flight. This test should be performed using extreme caution, preferably with a second operator controlling the GCS and able to intervene quickly if necessary. In order to reestablish control through the RC transmitter, the operator must first turn it back on and then toggle the flight mode selector.

/ TELEMETRY LINK LOSS

Some flight controllers will allow for the triggering of failsafe in the event that link is lost with the GCS through the telemetry module. This event will be triggered after a given period of time (10 seconds is usually adequate) and will result in either an immediate landing or the RTH action as predetermined by the user based on the operating environment. Like the RC Link Loss feature, some flight controllers will allow the user to specify whether Telemetry Link Loss during manual flight (control through the RC transmitter) will invoke failsafe. Telemetry Link Loss should be tested during autonomous flight by disconnecting the ground telemetry module from the GCS laptop or tablet and waiting the for link loss to take effect. An operator should be ready to take over with the RC transmitter in the event of an unintended maneuver.

Flight Test with Live Payload

Testing with a live payload may now begin. First, however, it may be necessary to perform a magnetometer calibration and/or RC range check due to the installation of metal or carbon structures that are part of the payload. Flight testing with a live payload may be used to verify that the aircraft maneuvers correctly with the gain values arrived at during flight testing, as well as to verify correct gimbal function and video transmitter range in various aircraft orientations.

PID Loops and Tuning

PID Loops

Almost all flight controllers utilize **proportional-integral-derivative (PID)** control loops in order to achieve control of the aircraft. These loops use a series of algorithms to apply motor and control surface changes to reduce the difference between the current state and the desired or commanded state. The **current state** refers to the condition of the aircraft as measured by the flight controller sensors (pitch and roll attitude, GPS position, ground speed, etc.). The **commanded state** refers to the condition of the aircraft required to execute its mission or maintain stable flight in its current mode (heading to next waypoint, straight-and-level flight orientation, mission altitude setting, etc.). The commanded state is received through inputs from the operator via the RC signal and/or via the autonomous flight mode scripts. The offset, the difference between the current and commanded state for a single aspect, is fed into a PID function, which outputs control outputs based on three numerical constants or gains: proportional (P), integral (I), and differential (D). These control outputs are sent to motors and control surfaces to produce changes in the current state of the aircraft, and these changes in turn are measured by the onboard sensors, the offset is

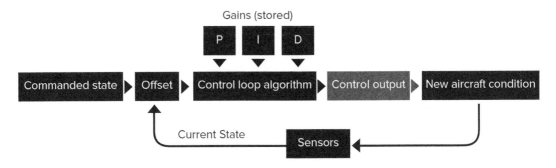

Figure 5-1. PID loop diagram.

updated, and the loop begins again (*Figure 5-1*). This process occurs many times per second, and each aspect of the aircraft (pitch, roll, yaw, etc.) executes a separate loop with unique PID gains. While the PID gains are considered constant in the mathematical sense, these gains may be changed by the operator, via the telemetry link, in order to produce better response. This process is referred to as tuning.

/ PROPORTIONAL GAIN

The proportional gain component is used to determine the aircraft's response proportionally to the offset. Hence, the larger the offset, the greater the response. Consider the gas pedal on a car. As you enter a highway and need to accelerate to match traffic (e.g., from 20 mph to 60 mph), you will depress the gas pedal more than when you accelerate from a stop (i.e., from 0 to 20 mph).

/ DIFFERENTIAL GAIN

The differential gain component is used to produce a response based on the rate of change in the offset. This provides a faster response to an increasing offset and to an abrupt disturbance. Differential gains can also be useful in reducing overshoot as the offset between the commanded and actual states closes. If we continue with our gas pedal analogy (introduced above in the Proportional Gain discussion), the differential gain would relate to how well a car accelerates. If you are driving uphill, you will most likely have to depress the gas pedal more in order to maintain a constant speed. If accelerating uphill, you will most likely need to depress the gas pedal even more and for a longer duration in order to reach the desired speed.

/ INTEGRAL GAIN

The integral gain component is used to vary the response by summing the offset over time. This is used to eliminate any residual offset in the system over time. Once again, consider driving a car uphill. If you misjudge the slope of the hill and the car is not able to accelerate as anticipated, the resulting persistent error will cause you to depress the gas pedal further.

Tuning Process

As previously discussed, each aspect of the aircraft's flight is controlled by a separate gain loop. Common loops available for tuning on most flight controllers are shown in Table 5-1.

Note that because a multicopter with a central CG is generally symmetrical about the pitch and roll axes, the gains for roll and pitch, as well as the roll rate and pitch rate, will usually be very similar.

Tuning is accomplished by providing the aircraft with step inputs about a single axis through the RC signal and observing the response of the aircraft. Appropriate gain values are very dependent on the weight distribution of the aircraft, so a dummy payload weight should be used during flight testing and tuning. A sealed sand bag can be used as a substitute for the payload during tuning.

Table 5-1. Common PID Tuning Loops on Flight Controllers

PARAMETERS	DESCRIPTION
Roll	Regulates the offset between the commanded and current **roll angle.**
Pitch	Regulates the offset between the commanded and current **pitch angle.**
Roll rate	Regulates the offset between the commanded and current **roll rate (angular velocity).**
Pitch rate	Regulates the offset between the commanded and current **pitch rate (angular velocity).**
Altitude	Regulates the offset between the commanded and current **altitude.**
Vertical climb rate	Regulates the offset between the commanded and current **climb rate.**
Yaw	Regulates the offset between the commanded and current **heading.**
Yaw rate	Regulates the offset between the commanded and current **yaw rate.**
Position	Regulates the offset between the commanded and current **latitude and longitude.**
Position rate	Regulates the offset between the commanded and current **translational velocity.**

CHAPTER SIX

Flight Operations

Mission Planning

ALTHOUGH DIFFERENT FLIGHT CONTROLLERS utilize different protocols for storing and executing missions, the general principles are fairly universal. An autonomous mission is essentially a list of commands that the flight controller reads through and executes in order one by one. These commands mostly consist of actions and waypoints. An action may or may not affect the way the aircraft moves through the air. Examples of actions include a command to a multicopter to maintain a constant heading or a command setting the camera-triggering interval. **Waypoints** consist of three-dimensional points in space defined by latitude, longitude, and altitude. A flight controller will maneuver the aircraft within predefined limitations (gains, pitch and roll, etc.) in order to pass within a specified distance of a waypoint. Certain types of waypoints may also have actions and options inherently associated with them. The underlined parameters are specified either in the aircraft configuration or in the options of the specific waypoint.

Fixed-Wing Commands

/ TAKE OFF

A take-off waypoint is the combination of a regular waypoint (the first of the mission) along with a Take Off action. It is important to understand that the aircraft does not necessarily need to be launched at the takeoff waypoint, but this waypoint specifies where the aircraft will navigate to after the Take Off action is completed. However, to avoid a stall, it is prudent for a fixed-wing aircraft to reach a safe altitude and airspeed during climb-out before attempting to maneuver. Therefore, the Take Off action will usually command the aircraft to maintain wings level and the current heading at the time of launch while attempting to reach a predefined **take-off speed**, **pitch**, and/or **climb rate**. The aircraft will continue operating within these parameters until reaching a predefined **safe altitude** or **breakout altitude**, which should be set safely above any obstacles in the immediate area as well as those between the launch position and the takeoff waypoint. At this point, the takeoff action is complete and the aircraft will maneuver to the take-off waypoint as it normally would. A fixed-wing aircraft will usually enter a circular loiter or orbit at the takeoff waypoint and climb up to the altitude specified for that waypoint prior to proceeding. Therefore, it is a good idea to place the takeoff waypoint over a safe open area where the aircraft can freely loiter and climb while the operator is able to observe it. It is also important to set the takeoff waypoint altitude safely above any obstacles in the area so that when the aircraft breaks the orbit to transit to the next waypoint, it can do so without risk.

/ LANDING

A landing waypoint normally defines the intended **touchdown point** of the aircraft. The **landing direction** may be defined either as an option within the waypoint or by the direction of the last leg before the landing waypoint. This vector should be aligned with the direction of the runway or landing area and also directed into the wind if possible. The user will usually need to define a **final approach glide slope**, which is the angle of the aircraft's descent path relative to the ground. Some flight controllers will allow a glide slope to be defined directly, whereas others will derive it from the distance between the landing waypoint and the previous waypoint (i.e., approach waypoint) as well as the altitude of that waypoint.

For example, if the two waypoints are 200 meters apart, and the altitude of the approach waypoint is 20 meters, glide slope and glideslope angle can be calculated as follows (*Figure 6-1*):

1. Determine glide slope as a percentage—rise over run:

$$\frac{20 \text{ meters}}{200 \text{ meters}} = 0.1 \text{ or } 10\% \text{ glide slope}$$

(or)

2. Determine glideslope angle using inverse tangent:

$$\tan^{-1} \frac{20 \text{ meters}}{200 \text{ meters}} = 5.7 \text{ degrees}$$

Most RC airplanes will have no problem achieving a 3–5 degree glide slope angle, or approximately 5–9% glide slope. A steeper glide slope will shorten the total landing distance but will incur more stress on the airframe, because more airspeed is translated to the vertical direction and the airplane will hit the ground harder. Airplanes with higher aspect ratios (long, skinny wings, not surprisingly like a glider) tend to "float," even with power off and especially in **ground effect**, and they may require flaps in order to make a steeper glide slope without risking stall. One of the best practices

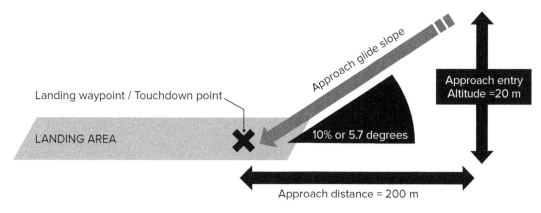

Figure 6-1. Glide slope calculation example.

for setting up an autonomous landing is to add a descending loiter to the end of the mission, which can be especially useful when operating in areas where terrain restricts flight at lower altitudes. This process will be described further at the end of this section.

Upon establishing itself on the glide slope, the flight controller will begin to execute a balancing act between achieving the desired glide slope and the **approach airspeed**, another parameter specified by the user. In a perfect world, this airspeed would translate directly to a descent rate that allows the glide slope to be maintained. However, air conditions as well as aircraft loading may discourage this; some flight controllers will allow the user to assign priority to one parameter over another. For example, if an aircraft has a significant margin between its approach speed and its stall speed, but obstacles in the approach path dictate a specific glide slope, the pilot may choose to assign a greater priority to that parameter. Ideally, the approach speed will be at least 25 percent higher than the stall speed.

The final parameters that the user must specify for an autonomous landing will define the flare behavior of the aircraft. A **flare** is a subtle maneuver that increases the airplane's angle of attack and is executed immediately before touchdown. It is meant to ensure landing while also reducing the descent rate in order to lessen stress on the airframe. A landing may be safely aborted prior to the flare point, but after that point, the aircraft is, in a sense, committed to the landing. As such, the flare point is normally defined by a **flare altitude**. Once the aircraft descends through the flare altitude, the flight controller will normally attempt to maintain a wings-level attitude and constant heading within the constraint of a predetermined **landing roll limit**, cut the throttle to idle (or a user-specified **flare throttle setting**), and attempt to maintain a specific **touchdown pitch**. This touchdown pitch will vary between aircraft, but between 0 and 5 degrees is usually a good starting value, adjusting as necessary to achieve the desired vertical speed at touchdown without risking a stall. If the aircraft is consistently hitting the ground too hard but not stalling, increase the touchdown pitch by a degree and reevaluate.

Similarly, many of the fixed-wing landing parameters, especially the flare terms, should be determined experimentally during flight testing. In a large open area, experiment with these parameters until a satisfactory landing is repeatable. Then record the following, which will be relatively constant for most operations:

1. Final approach glide slope
2. Approach speed
3. Flare altitude
4. Flare throttle setting
5. Touchdown pitch
6. Flare point distance: Once a satisfactory flare altitude is determined, the flare point distance may be determined by using the GCS software to measure the distance between the landing waypoint and the observed flare point position.

Note that many fixed-wing aircraft that come with flight controllers integrated and designed for use with specific GCS software will likely simplify the landing process, as they have undergone flight testing by the manufacture in order to lock down many of the parameters mentioned above. Such a system may only require the operator to designate an intended touchdown point and an approach corridor free of obstacles within the glide slope path of the aircraft. The aircraft will then execute the landing based on this glide slope as well as specific approach speeds, flare altitude, and flare throttle and pitch settings. More sophisticated systems may be capable of selecting from multiple user-defined approach corridors based on wind direction as detected by the aircraft. Meanwhile, less sophisticated systems may rely on a spiral landing at an operator-determined point, similar to a fixed-wing Land Now maneuver.

Landing Procedure

Using the values above, consider the following suggested landing procedure for mission planning (*Figure 6-2*):

1. Determine the prevailing wind direction in order to determine the landing approach path. Land into the wind whenever possible.
2. Identify any obstacles in the landing approach path. Determine the height of each obstacle and a minimum safe altitude above the obstacle.
   Example: A 10-meter-tall tree is located off the approach end of the runway. A minimum safe altitude above this obstacle should be 1.5 to 2 times the height of the obstacle, as appropriate, which gives a safe clearance altitude of 15 meters.

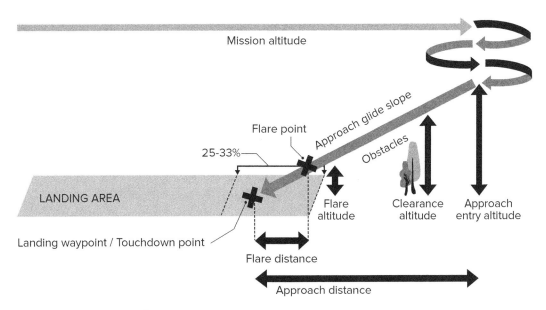

Figure 6-2. Landing procedure.

3. Divide the minimum safe clearance altitude by the tangent of the intended glide slope in order to determine the appropriate location of the landing waypoint (touchdown point).

   Example: Assuming a 7 degree glide slope:

   $$\left(\frac{15 \text{ meters}}{\tan{(7 \text{ deg})}} \right) = 123 \text{ meters}$$

   The chart in Figure 6-3 may also be used to make such estimates in the following steps.

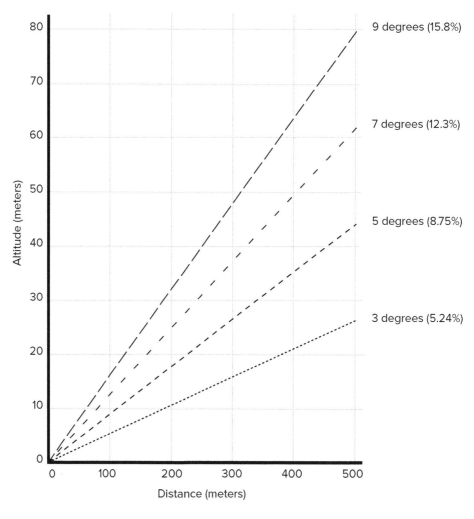

Figure 6-3. Glide slope (altitude vs. distance) for estimating clearance altitude, flare altitude, and approach entry altitude.

4. Use the GCS software to place the estimated touchdown point: Starting from the obstacle along the approach path, measure the distance derived in step 3 to the landing area. Ideally, this touchdown point should be located within the first 25 to 33% of the runway. Adjust the glide slope as necessary (which may require the use of flaps) in order to achieve a safe approach.

   Example: Find the obstacle on the satellite map in the flight planning tool of the GCS software. From this point, draw a 123-meter line toward the runway. If this line does not reach the runway, then the aircraft is capable of achieving the minimum obstacle clearance altitude while also making a safe landing on the selected glide slope. If the line extends beyond the safe landing area, then the glide slope will need to be adjusted in order to make a safe approach.

5. Verify the position and altitude of the flare point. Ideally, this flare point will be located at the approach end or threshold of the runway or landing area. This placement theoretically will reduce the chances of the aircraft touching down short of the intended landing area.

   Example: Once again using the GCS software, measure the distance between the landing waypoint and the approach end of the runway. Multiplying this distance by the decimal value of the final approach glide slope will determine the proper flare altitude in order to flare at this position. The flare point distance and altitude should be more or less constant for most operations using a given glide slope.

6. If necessary, add a descending loiter waypoint in order to set up the approach. This is recommended when operating in an area where terrain will limit operations at low altitude. Begin by locating a safe position along the approach path where the aircraft may descend from the mission altitude in order to enter the approach. This waypoint (or set of waypoints) will also serve as the approach waypoint.

7. Measure the distance between the landing waypoint and the intended loiter/approach waypoint. This will serve as the approach distance.

8. Determine the approach entry altitude by multiplying the approach distance by the glide slope decimal.

   Example: You have determined an approach distance of approximately 400 meters.
   400 meters x 0.123 = 49.2 meters

9. Configure the approach waypoint with a safe loiter radius and a final target altitude that matches the approach entry altitude. When properly configured, the aircraft will fly to the approach waypoint at the mission altitude. There, the aircraft will enter a circular loiter and descend to the approach entry altitude. This loiter will allow the aircraft to descend more quickly while also covering less distance and avoiding the surrounding terrain.

Rotor-Wing Commands

/ TAKE OFF

Similar to the fixed-wing command, a rotor-wing take-off waypoint is a regular waypoint preceded by a Take-Off action. It is important to understand that the aircraft does not necessarily need to be launched at the takeoff waypoint but this waypoint specifies where the aircraft will navigate to after the takeoff action is completed. Once armed, the aircraft will attempt to maintain its GPS position while increasing upward thrust in order to meet a predetermined **take-off climb rate**. The result is a straight up vertical climb until reaching a predefined **safe altitude** or **breakout altitude**. At this point, the Take Off action is complete and the aircraft will maneuver to the take-off waypoint as normal. It is important to set the takeoff waypoint altitude safely above any obstacles in the area so that when the aircraft transits to the next waypoint, it can do so without risk.

/ LANDING

A rotor-wing landing waypoint will be executed as a regular waypoint followed by a Landing action. The aircraft will maneuver to the waypoint and then attempt to maintain the waypoint's GPS position while decreasing thrust in order to reach a predefined **landing descent rate**. The result is a straight down vertical descent. Some flight controllers, after descending through a **final landing transition altitude**, will attempt to slow the descent of the aircraft to a **final landing descent rate** in order to achieve a softer touchdown. Below this transition point, the flight controller may also limit the attitude range of the aircraft in an attempt to touchdown in as level an orientation as possible. This behavior tends to de-prioritize position accuracy and may cause the aircraft to be pushed off target in breezy conditions. Therefore, if the final landing transition altitude is programmable, it should be set low enough to avoid significant drift during the final stage while high enough to allow the aircraft to safely slow to the final landing descent rate before contacting the ground.

Most flight controllers will employ a ground detection feature, which allows it to recognize that it has landed based on the IMU detecting a failure to descend in spite of continually decreasing thrust, and it will disarm the motor(s). While useful, this feature must be properly tuned; if ground detection is not sensitive enough, it will take longer to disarm and the aircraft may tip over. If ground detection is too sensitive, it may be triggered by normal maneuvers, which may cause the aircraft to disarm the motors in flight and, in rare cases, drop out of the sky. It is usually best to start flight testing with the ground detection feature at a less-sensitive setting, and configure an RC transmitter kill switch in order to stop the motors if the aircraft starts to tip.

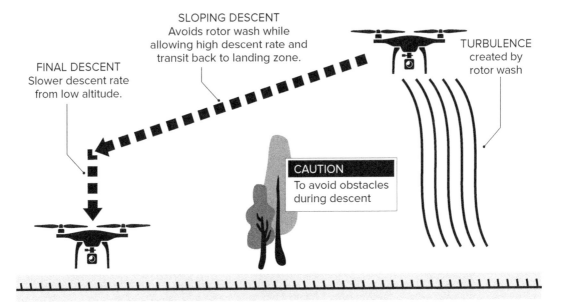

SLOPING DESCENT
Avoids rotor wash while
allowing high descent rate and
transit back to landing zone.

TURBULENCE
created by
rotor wash

FINAL DESCENT
Slower descent rate
from low altitude.

CAUTION
To avoid obstacles
during descent

Figure 6-4. Rotor wash and a sloping descent.

Rotor-wing aircraft are notoriously bad at straight-down descents because the aircraft passes through its own **rotor wash**, the turbulence generated just below the aircraft by the spinning of the blades. This rotor wash can lead to violent oscillations that the flight controller may not be able to handle properly. One solution is to decrease the descent rate, but this leads to very long descents from high altitudes, which is not an efficient use of valuable flight time. The best course of action is to execute an enroute sloping descent from the previous waypoint to a minimum safe landing altitude (5–10 meters, depending on the aircraft), thus avoiding rotor wash and reducing the distance of the vertical descent during landing. It is, however, critical to plan this descent so as to avoid obstacles (*Figure 6-4*).

/ REGION OF INTEREST (ROI)

Regions of interest (ROIs), which are very similar to waypoints, are specified within a flight plan and consist of a latitude, longitude, and usually altitude. However, rather than having the aircraft fly to an ROI, a rotor-wing aircraft, when commanded, will point its nose and/or camera/gimbal at the ROI while continuing to execute the flight plan. ROIs may be used to gather video footage of an object on the ground while flying around it.

Common Actions

/ LOITER

The loiter action is intended to hold an aircraft at a waypoint. A rotor-wing aircraft will simply hover at a given waypoint, whereas a fixed-wing aircraft will orbit the waypoint, usually in a specified direction and/or at a specified radius. Users may usually also specify the length of time for which the aircraft will loiter or command the aircraft to loiter indefinitely, until it is commanded into another action by the user. The loiter action can be used to hold a fixed-wing aircraft in position while a landing approach is created or to allow FPV payloads to gather footage from a fixed perspective.

/ PHOTO SURVEY

Photo surveys may be used for gathering agricultural, surveying, and mapping data in the form of multiple still images that are stitched together using post-processing software to create high-resolution 2D or 3D mosaics. Photo surveys are usually inserted into a flight plan as if they were a single waypoint, but in reality they are composed of a collection of many waypoints that achieve the effect of guiding the aircraft back and forth in a grid pattern across a specified area while triggering a camera payload. This survey pattern is often referred to as a lawnmower or Zamboni pattern, drawing a comparison to the way those vehicles crisscross back and forth over an area.

Users begin by specifying the area they wish to survey, usually in the form of a polygon drawn in the GCS over the satellite map. When converted to a photo survey, the GCS will then auto-populate this area with parallel photo survey legs, each compromised of multiple camera trigger waypoints (*Figure 6-5*). Depending on the GCS software and flight controller system being used, these camera trigger points may be based on triggering the camera either at a specific GPS position or at a constant interval and aircraft speed. Most GCS software will allow these parallel legs to be rotated to a user-specified heading.

Next, the user will input data regarding the specific camera being used (focal length, resolution, aspect ratio, etc.) as well as the required resolution for the images being gathered, commonly referred to as **ground sample distance (GSD)**. GSD is the distance between adjacent individual pixels in a photo of the Earth's surface. The smaller the distance between centers of pixels, the higher the resolution of the image. With a given camera, GSD will increase (and resolution will decrease) as the altitude increases. A lower GSD means that individual pixels represent a smaller area of the Earth's surface and greater detail is being captured, which can be beneficial for when images are stitched together. As such, the required GSD and camera data will determine the altitude at which the photo survey must be flown, as well as the lateral separation between grid pattern paths and the interval for triggering of the camera.

Most GCS software will allow the user to refine the placement of photo survey legs and camera trigger points in order to optimize image collection and, in turn, post-processing output. Photo survey flight plans are generated primarily based on the ground sample distance and the desired overlap of the images produced. In many cases, GCS software will calculate GSD based on the following inputs from the operator: camera focal length, sensor dimensions, and sensor pixel dimensions. The user may then adjust the altitude of the photo survey (within the limitations of legality and surface obstacles) in order to achieve the desired GSD, which is driven by the application and post-processing software.

The user may further refine the lateral separation between grid paths and the camera-trigger interval by adjusting the desired overlap between images that will be adjacent when stitched together. Overlap refers to the area on the Earth's surface that is covered by both of two adjacent images. This parameter is usually expressed as a percentage, with a higher percentage denoting a greater overlap, and most GCS software will allow the user to specify both endlap and sidelap. **Endlap** governs the distance between sequential camera trigger points within a photo survey and thus the number of these points within a leg. **Sidelap** determines the distance between photo survey legs and thus the number of legs within a photo survey. Increasing endlap will create more camera trigger points within each leg (since the trigger points are closer together), while increasing sidelap will place photo survey legs closer together and

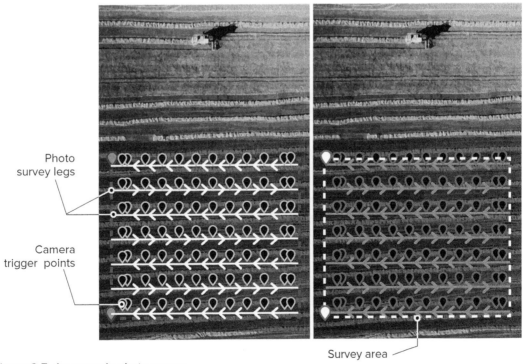

Figure 6-5. An example photo survey.

potentially increase the number of legs required to survey a given area. Like GSD, ideal overlap values will depend on application and post-processing software. Greater overlap can provide better-quality mosaics when stitched together but will also increase the number of parallel paths required to survey a given area, thus increasing the flight time required to complete the photo survey. The number of photos produced will also increase with an increase in overlap, which can drive up processing time exponentially. Furthermore, greater endlap will require more rapid camera triggering, which is limited to approximately one second in most cameras; thus, the aircraft may require a slower flight speed (which some fixed-wing aircraft may not be capable of).

To summarize, the steps to create a photo survey are:

1. Determine heights of obstacles within the survey area.
2. Insert photo survey into flight plan in GCS.
3. Define the photo survey area in the GCS.
4. Verify that camera parameters (focal length, sensor dimensions, and sensor pixel dimensions) are properly entered into the GCS.
5. Adjust the photo survey altitude to achieve the desired GSD while avoiding obstacles and illegal airspace.
6. Verify the overlap parameter(s) in the GCS.
7. Check flight time and number of camera trigger events as reported by the GCS.

Following are some additional notes on photo surveys:

- Obviously, the execution of photo survey actions is heavily dependent on the flight controller having a means of triggering the camera (as discussed under Imaging Sensor Payloads in Chapter 1).

- Some GCS software will allow users to specify a start and/or end leg for a photo survey. This allows a partially completed photo survey to be resumed following an interruption due to a failsafe (such as a low battery).

- The user will usually be able to rotate the heading of the photo survey legs in the GCS software based on actual wind conditions. Flying the photo survey legs with a crosswind (photo survey legs perpendicular to the wind) will usually result in more balanced battery use throughout the flight as well as greater battery efficiency.

- Rotor-wing and fixed-wing photo surveys are fundamentally the same, but fixed-wing aircraft may require additional maneuvering space to turn around at the end of one path and become established on the next path.

- Some post-processing software allows the option to use information encoded in the flight controller logs recording the time, the aircraft's position, and the aircraft's attitude when each photo was taken. This information is tagged to a digital image file in what is called EXIF data.

/ LOOP

A Loop action is used to return an aircraft to a specified previous waypoint in order to repeat a flight plan (or a portion of one). Some flight control software will allow the user to specify the number of times that an aircraft should loop back to a previous waypoint before moving on, while others may require user intervention in order to break the loop. A loop may be used to collect multiple data sets or video shots over a constant path. Placing an aircraft in a looping box pattern during flight testing is also a great, repeatable way to observe changes in behavior caused by tuning gains.

Developing a Checklist

Power Off Preflight Checks

1. **Check all battery levels and conditions before each mission.**
   Five batteries:

   i. Aircraft

   ii. RC transmitter

   iii. Aircraft interface devices (laptop, tablet, phone, etc.)

   iv. Payload

   v. Payload interface devices (video monitor, video receiver, etc.)

2. **Check and confirm that aircraft structures are secure and not damaged.**
   Fixed-wing:

   - Wings
   - Horizontal tail
   - Vertical tail

   Remember: It is common for the wings and/or parts of the empennage of fixed-wing airframes to be removed or folded for easy transport. It is important to verify that these structures are inspected for proper connection as well as for regular preventative maintenance.

   Multicopter:

   - Arms
   - Landing gear skids

   Remember: It is common for the arms and/or landing gear of multicopter airframes to be removed or folded for easy transport. It is important to verify that these structures are inspected for proper connection as well as for regular preventative maintenance.

3. **Check that all motors are secure in their mounts.**

4. **Check that all motors spin freely and are clear of dirt and debris.**
A motor that does not spin freely may be an indication of damage or malfunction. This is also an opportunity to check that the propeller spin arcs are not obstructed by wiring or any other structure.

5. **Check that all propellers are securely mounted to their corresponding motor shafts.**
Fixed-wing: Ensure that the propeller spin direction is correct and that folding propeller blades are secured yet free to deploy.
Multicopter: Ensure that propeller spin directions are correct for each motor.

6. **Check that the propeller blades are not damaged.**
Feel along the leading edges of the blades and out to the tips for knicks, cracks, and deformities.

7. **Check that all servos are securely mounted and free of dirt and debris.**

8. **Check that all servo linkages are secure.**
Inspect:
   - Servo horns—Secured to servo and free of damage
   - Servo horn rod linkage—Secured to servo horn and free to rotate
   - Control rod—Secure and free of damage
   - Control surface linkage—Secured to control surface horn and free to rotate
   - Control surface horn—Secured to control surface and free of damage

9. **Check that all control surfaces are free to move.**
Gently apply pressure to the linkage rod to check the range of motion of the control surface. Remember that servos can be easily damage if mishandled.

10. **Check control surfaces for damage.**
Pay special attention to possible cracks developing along the control surface hinges. This can be accomplished by gently pulling backward on the control surface while looking for daylight along the hinge and feeling for play.

11. **Check that all components and wires are secured and free of damage.**
Inspect for chaffing, pinching, and exposed conductors.

12. **Check that all connectors are secure.**
   - Double-check connections that are commonly disconnected for transport, and verify proper connection and port selection.
   - Verify that crimps are in good condition and not exposed.
   - Verify that all connectors are fully inserted into their corresponding ports.
   - Check locking or clip connectors by gently tugging on them.
   - Check that SD card(s) are properly installed.

13. **Check that the GPS/compass mast is ready for flight and secure.**
    This is another component commonly removed or folded for transport.

14. **Check the airspeed sensor system.**
    - Check the pitot tube mount assembly.
    - Check for dirt and debris. Pitot tubes, especially those mounted under the wing, can often become clogged by dirt during landing.
    - Verify that any air pressure lines are properly connected, secured, and free of damage.

15. **Inspect the camera gimbal/mount.**
    - Check to ensure that the gimbal/mount is secured to the aircraft.
    - Check the condition and integrity of vibration dampeners.
    - Check that the gimbal/mount is free to move, unobstructed by wires and debris.
    - Check that all wires are properly connected, secured, and free of damage.

16. **Check the camera memory card.**
    Verify that a memory card with an appropriate amount of available space is properly installed in the camera.

17. **Check that the camera is properly installed.**
    - Verify that the camera is securely mounted on the gimbal/mount.
    - Check that the gimbal/mount is properly balanced with the camera installed.
    - Verify that all camera wires are properly connected, secured, and free of damage.

18. **Check the camera lens.**
    - Remove the lens cover from the camera.
    - Verify that the lens is free of damage and debris.

19. **Check that the battery is securely installed (not yet connected).**

20. **Check that the aircraft center of gravity (CG) with the battery and payload installed is appropriate.**
    The CG is the point about which the aircraft will balance if suspended.

    Fixed-wing: Most airframes will include some indication of the proper CG location, either indicated on the aircraft or in its documentation. The CG should be as close as practically possible to this recommended location along the aircraft's nose–tail centerline. If in doubt, a forward CG will result in a more stable aircraft.

    Multicopter: The CG of a multicopter should be positioned directly below the center of an imaginary circle passing through the propeller mounts of all of the motors. A lower CG in this location, usually the result of low-slung payloads and batteries, will result in a more stable yet less maneuverable multicopter.

Power On Procedure

At any time after power is connected, the propellers have the potential to spin and control surfaces have the potential to move. Best safety practices dictate that personnel keep all body parts clear of propeller arcs and control surface pinch points while the power is on.

1. **Power ON the camera and verify the operating mode.**
   It is important to power on the camera and verify it is functioning correctly before powering on the aircraft and the gimbal to avoid putting undue stress on the gimbal motors.

2. **Verify that the throttle (usually the left stick on the RC transmitter) is in the down or idle position and all switches are in their start-up/safe positions.**
   Examples of start-up/safe positions include:
   - Flight mode: Stabilize
   - Landing gear: Down
   - MUX: RC control

3. **Power ON the RC transmitter; check voltage and model.**
   Once again verify that the RC transmitter is not likely to lose power during flight. Also verify that the transmitter is properly configured for the specific aircraft, as many transmitters support multiple model configurations. Powering on the RC transmitter before the aircraft ensures that positive control is established and prevents unexpected control surface deflections or the possibility of invoking a failsafe condition.

4. **Place the aircraft on a level surface and connect the battery to the aircraft's battery lead.**
   Look for status lights on components to indicate they are powering on correctly. Be prepared to disconnect power immediately if you see smoke, sparks, or unexpected behavior of mechanical components.

5. **Leave the aircraft level and undisturbed while the system initializes as required.**
   IMUs in the flight controller or gimbal control unit (GCU) may require an initialization period under stationary conditions.

6. **Connect the aircraft to the GCS via the telemetry module.**
   If a link cannot be established, first check telemetry module connections and status indicators (LEDs on the air and/or ground telemetry module, indicators in the GCS software, etc.). Then **cycle power** on the aircraft and restart the GCS software as necessary.

Power On Preflight Checks

1. **Check alerts.**
   The GCS will display indications of failures that might prevent the aircraft from being armed.

2. **Check signal strength for all emitters.**
   - RC Transmitter—Perform range check and reconfigure antennas as necessary.
   - Telemetry—Reconfigure antennas as necessary.
   - Video—Reconfigure antennas as necessary.

3. **Check sensors.**
   GPS—Verify that the GPS module is properly connected to the flight controller and that it is beginning to acquire satellites. Once 3D fix is established, verify that the GPS position indicated on the moving map reflects the aircraft's actual location and responds correctly in real time. Excessive drift in the GPS position after 3D fix may indicate a failure.

   Compass—Check that the compass heading on the moving map accurately reflects the actual heading of the aircraft and responds correctly in real time. Excessive or constant drift in magnetic heading could indicate improper calibration. It is important to perform compass calibration at the beginning of each new flying day and at each different flying location. Magnetic fields can vary greatly between geographic locations and near sources of manmade interference.

   Accelerometer/IMU—Check that the attitude displayed on the artificial horizon accurately reflects the aircraft's actual attitude and responds correctly in real time. If the artificial horizon does not indicate level when the aircraft is placed on a level surface, or the artificial horizon drifts, then a recalibration may be required. Crashes or hard landings often necessitate recalibration.

   Airspeed sensor—The airspeed sensor should be zeroed via the GCS software before flight while the aircraft is stationary. It is best to zero the airspeed sensor while using a hand to loosely cover it, preventing any wind from disturbing the readings. Then, blowing into the pitot tube should produce a positive indicated airspeed response in real time, and the airspeed should return to approximately zero after air stops moving over it. If the airspeed does not respond appropriately, the pitot tube and accompanying pressure tubing may be improperly connected, damaged, or clogged. Sealing the front opening of a pitot tube with a fingertip may be used to check for leaks in the system. While this opening is tightly covered, you should see the airspeed reading rise as pressure builds, eventually leveling off. This airspeed reading should return to zero when the finger is removed. If airspeed is not maintained, this may be an indication of a leak between the pitot tube and the airspeed sensor.

4. **Review flight plans.**
   - Check that the appropriate flight plan is uploaded to the aircraft.
   - Verify that flight plan altitudes, flight paths, and recovery points are appropriate based on obstacles and hazards in the field.
   - Check the estimated flight time.

5. **Verify failsafe settings.**
   - Check the failsafe switch function.
   - Check RC transmitter Link Loss function.
   - Check that failsafe altitudes are set high enough to avoid all obstacles in the field.
   - Check the Low Battery Voltage setting and action.
   - Review other failsafe settings.
   - Check that geofence settings are appropriate based on altitude limits, obstacles, and hazards in the field.

6. **Verify control response.**
   - Check that RC main sticks are configured correctly and not reversed.
   - Verify that the flight mode switch is properly configured based on mission.
   - Check that all other RC switches are properly assigned and not reversed.
   - Check proper control surface and motor responses based on RC inputs.
   - Check control surface limits for servo binding and linkage rod flex.
   - Check proper control surface response in stabilize flight mode.
   - Check transition between flight controller authority and MUX, if installed.

7. **Check electrical system.**
   - Check battery voltage.
   - Perform PMU calibration as necessary using a battery checker.
   - Check major electrical components for excessive heat.

Arming and Launch

1. **Verify GCS.**
   - Verify that the GCS software is running properly.
   - Verify that cached maps for the flight area have loaded correctly.
   - Verify that appropriate tabs and menus are selected.

2. **Secure the access hatch(es).**
   - Secure any loose cables.
   - Install access hatches and verify that they will not detach in the airstream.
3. **Stow the camera (as necessary).**
   - In some cases, fixing the camera forward for takeoff allows it to act as a pilot cam.
   - The camera may need to be stowed in a certain orientation in order to prevent lens damage or dust build-up during takeoff.
4. **Verify that all aircraft, vehicles, and personnel are clear of the takeoff and operations areas.**
   - 10 meters is a reasonable safe distance for most operations.
   - All personnel should maintain visual contact with the aircraft while it is in the immediate area, to ensure they are prepared in the event of unexpected maneuvers.
5. **Move aircraft to the intended launch/home position.**
   In some cases, this is the point to which the aircraft will return if a failsafe landing is required.
6. **Verify that the throttle control is set to its minimum position.**
7. **Disable aircraft onboard safety, if applicable.**
   Some flight controller systems incorporate a pushbutton that is mounted to the airframe and used to prevent inadvertent arming.
8. **Verify that all crewmembers are clear of the aircraft and ready to launch.**
   Fixed-wing:
   - It is essential that the pilot has good communication with both the GCS operator and anyone involved in launching the aircraft.
   - The motor, when running at the takeoff setting, will be noisy; therefore, the launching plan should be discussed in advance.
9. **Verify that the flight mode is correct.**
   - Verify the flight mode switch position.
   - Confirm that the flight mode is repeated in the GCS.
10. **Arm the aircraft.**
    - Look for GCS messages indicating conditions that may prevent arming.
    Multicopter:
    - Most flight controllers arm either through the GCS or by inputting a specified command through the RC transmitter sticks.
    - If executing an auto launch, be prepared to abort or kill if any motors fail to start up properly.

11. **Perform control checks as necessary.**

    Fixed-wing:

    - Perform final checks of control surface movement and flap position.
    - Check motor function by running it up to full throttle while the aircraft is securely held.
    - During the motor test, look for excessive vibrations or any excessive strain on the structure.

    Rotor-wing:

    - Check vehicle pitch, roll, yaw, and collective control while in a low hover.
    - Check GPS position accuracy by briefly switching to a GPS stabilize mode.

12. **Observe takeoff and climb for failures.**

    Fixed-wing:

    - Look for signs that the aircraft is struggling to maintain a positive rate of climb.
    - Observe the aircraft's ability to maintain takeoff heading.
    - Observe the aircraft's response to the wind.
    - Look for excessive voltage drop or current draw.
    - Be prepared to abort if necessary.

    Rotor-wing:

    - Look for signs that the aircraft is struggling to maintain a positive rate of climb.
    - Observe the aircraft's ability to maintain GPS position.
    - Observe the aircraft's response to the wind.
    - Look for excessive voltage drop or current draw.
    - Be prepared to abort if necessary.

13. **Retract landing gear.**

    Fixed-wing:

    - Verify visually that landing the gear retracts fully.
    - If one or more of the landing gear fails to retract, cycle the landing gear switch. If this is unsuccessful, consider aborting the mission. Added drag may adversely affect flight performance and endurance.

    Rotor-wing:

    - Unless necessary for a panning camera shot, it is best to leave the landing gear extended in the event of a lost link failsafe procedure. It can be prudent to conduct a dry run of these types of camera maneuvers with the landing gear deployed while monitoring link quality in the GCS.

- If retracting the landing gear is required, verify visually that the landing gear fully retracts. If one or more of the landing gear fails to retract, cycle the landing gear switch. If this does not correct the issue, RTH, land, and attempt to remedy the problem.

In Flight

1. **The GCS operator and pilot must maintain constant communication regarding aircraft status and in order to establish positive exchange of control of the aircraft from one to another.**
   An example of a positive exchange of control:

   GCS OPERATOR: We need to get a more dynamic shot. I need you to take control of the aircraft.

   PILOT: Roger, taking control in GPS stabilize.

   GCS OPERATOR: Roger, I see you have control in GPS stabilize. Your aircraft. Aircraft is pointed to your left, straight and level, altitude 20 meters, airspeed 5 meters per second.

   PILOT: Roger, my aircraft. I see proper response.

2. **The pilot maintains visual contact with the aircraft and is prepared to intervene and take control if necessary.**

3. **The pilot attempts to match RC transmitter stick settings with an aircraft in autonomous mode in the event that the pilot must take control.**
   When in doubt, pitch/roll/yaw: neutral; throttle: mid.

4. **The GCS operator constantly monitors aircraft status.**
   - Altitude—Loss of altitude could indicate a failure.
   - Airspeed—Abrupt changes could indicate turbulence or wind. Loss of airspeed could indicate a failure.
   - Flight mode—Will indicate RTH, loss of GPS, or other failsafe conditions.
   - Voltage—Indicates flight time remaining and battery health.
   - Current—Indicates power draw by motors and potential failures.
   - Alerts—Indicate potential failures observed by the flight controller.
   - Position—Aircraft is properly following intended flight path.

5. **In the event of a loss of telemetry downlink or suspected crash, note the aircraft's last known position, altitude, and heading.**
   This information may help the pilot locate the aircraft visually or aid in recovering a downed aircraft.

Recovery and Shutdown

1. **Advise all personnel that the aircraft is returning to the field.**
   All personnel should maintain visual contact with the aircraft while it is in the immediate area in case of unexpected maneuvers.

2. **Lower landing gear.**
   Fixed-wing:
   - Visually verify that the landing gear extends fully.
   - If one or more of the landing gear fails to extend, cycle the landing gear switch. If this is unsuccessful, it is usually safest to execute a belly landing on a soft surface with the landing gear up and the propeller stopped before touchdown.

   Rotor-wing:
   - Visually verify that the landing gear extends fully.
   - If one or more of the landing gear fails to extend, cycle the landing gear switch. If this is unsuccessful, it may be possible to recover a small aircraft by hand (essentially grabbing it out of the air from beneath while it is descending). In this case, however, the pilot must be ready to climb immediately if the situation becomes unsafe, or to kill the motors as soon as the aircraft is successfully recovered.
   - If the landing gear fails to extend and you attempt a surface landing while carrying a camera payload, try to land on a soft surface. Be prepared to kill the motors as soon as the aircraft contacts the ground. The aircraft will come to rest on its booms and motor mounts—potentially damaging motor mounts, motors, booms, and propellers—but the goal is to prevent damage to the camera and gimbal. If not carrying a camera payload, attempt a normal landing on a soft surface with the landing gear up.

3. **Stow the camera, if necessary.**
   - In some cases, fixing the camera forward for landing allows it to act as a pilot cam.
   - Cameras may need to be stowed in a certain orientation in order to prevent lens damage or dust build-up during landing.

4. **Verify that the intended recovery area is clear of people and obstacles.**
   If possible, the pilot cam may be used to look for obstacles in the approach path, such as trees, power lines, and aerial cables.

5. **Observe the aircraft as it approaches the recovery area.**

   The pilot must be prepared to take control if necessary.

   Fixed-wing: One not-so-intuitive lesson from RC flying is that, in order to correct an adverse condition during landing, a pilot should apply pitch for airspeed and power for altitude. At the low speeds required for landing, pitching the nose upward to increase altitude (which is a common gut reaction) may produce a stall, which is very difficult to recover from at the final approach altitude. Instead, apply immediate full throttle and maintain a wings-level climb until the aircraft is at a safe altitude to execute further maneuvers. It is a good idea for a pilot observing an autonomous landing to set the RC throttle stick to the full throttle position, which will immediately command a climb if the pilot must take over control. The act of a fixed-wing aircraft climbing to abort a landing is referred to as a **wave-off**, which normally necessitates the execution of the equally creatively named **go-around**. In a go-around, the aircraft is returned to final approach in order to attempt another landing.

   Rotor-wing: When a rotor-wing aircraft descends vertically, it tends to pass through the turbulence generated by its own spinning propeller blades, referred to as rotor wash. This can produce violent oscillations that wreak havoc on the flight controller and have the potential to crash the aircraft. This can be remedied by decreasing the aircraft's descent rate, sometimes to near a snail's pace. Often, a better alternative for descending from a high altitude is to execute a gradient descent. This is accomplished at the end of a mission by having the aircraft begin descending to a safe landing altitude (e.g., 5–10 meters) while simultaneously moving to the landing site, being careful to avoid obstacles. Once there, the aircraft can begin a slow vertical descent to the ground for landing. A pilot observing oscillations during vertical descent should be prepared to take manual control and immediately slow the descent.

6. **Once the aircraft comes to rest on the ground, set throttle to the lowest position and disarm the aircraft.**

   Rotor-wing: Be prepared to kill the motors immediately if a tip-over is observed or expected.

7. **Approach the aircraft with caution.**

   Make sure to keep all body parts clear of the propellers at all times.

8. **Activate the aircraft's onboard safety.**

   In most cases, a pushbutton may be used to forcibly kill the motors in the event that the aircraft fails to disarm by normal means. Only attempt this if it can be done safely. The use of an RC transmitter kill switch is preferable.

9. **Remove the access hatch and disconnect the battery, or download data as necessary.**

10. **Power the camera OFF and install the lens cover.**

11. **Check for damage, debris, and excessive heat.**

    Make a note of any damage that will require repair before the next flight. Pay special attention to propellers, control surfaces, wing tips, and landing gear.

    Multicopter: Carefully feel the heat of each motor and ESC. These components should be warm but not scalding. They also should be at approximately the same temperature. Uneven or excessive heating could be an indication of improper CG placement or potential failure of that component.

Building a Field Kit

BEYOND THE GROUND SUPPORT equipment required for regular flight operations—such as launchers, generators, flight batteries, etc.—a field kit consists of tools, materials, and equipment that allow operators to complete regular repairs and maintenance while in the field. Following is a list of what should be included in a comprehensive field kit.

Basic Tools:

- Screwdriver set
- Allen wrench set
- Plier set
- Socket wrench set
- Adjustable wrench
- Forceps
- Hobby knife or razor

Electrical Equipment:

- Wire cutter/stripper
- Crimp tool
- Battery checker
- Battery charger
- Charging leads or octopus (two for each type of connector in use)
- Power source (auto inverter)
- Multimeter
- Extension cords

Programming Equipment:

- USB cables
- ESC programming card (with appropriate adapters)
- Servo tester (with appropriate adapters)

Repair Materials and Consumables:

- Clamps
- Foam-safe CA glue with kicker
- Duct tape
- Double-sided foam tape
- Electrical tape
- Velcro tape and straps
- Dual lock tape
- Cable ties and tie-downs
- Crimps and appropriate connectors
- Rubbing alcohol or alcohol swabs
- Threadlocker
- Small amount of appropriate fastening hardware in sectioned container

Spares and Replacements:

- Servo connector cables
- Motors (ready for installation)
- ESCs (ready for installation)
- Servos (ready for installation)
- Servo horns
- Servo rods (ready for installation)
- Propellers
- Propeller adapters
- Spinners
- Video transmitter and receiver
- RC transmitter batteries
- Payload/video system batteries
- AA and AAA batteries (as necessary)
- Laptop and/or tablet charger

Comfort/Productivity:

- Folding table
- Folding chairs
- Tent or shade
- Fixed-wing aircraft stand (if necessary)

Safety Gear:

- Trauma kit (suited for lacerations, burns, and shock)
- Fire extinguisher
- Two-way radios
- Handheld weather station
- Eye protection
- Ear protection
- Gloves (for hand launch and/or crash recovery)
- Rubber gloves (for both emergencies and repairs)
- Sunscreen and sun protection
- Insect repellent
- Bottled water
- Flashlights, lanterns, and/or headlamps
- High-visibility vests
- Safety cones or barriers

Glossary

accelerometer. *See* inertial measurement unit (IMU).

airfoil. The shape of the two-dimensional cross section of a wing or lifting surface when viewed from the tip. This shape, which could be described as an elongated teardrop, produces lift by creating higher pressure along its bottom surface than its top when air moves around it.

angle of attack. The angle between the direction of the moving air mass that encounters the wing and the chord line of that wing.

approach airspeed. The airspeed that a fixed-wing aircraft will attempt to maintain during the approach phase of a landing action.

articulating mount. A payload mount that attaches the camera or sensor to a movable tray and uses a pair of servos or other actuators to keep the camera pointed downward relative to the Earth (referred to as the Nadir position), which may improve the quality of certain data sets.

autonomous flight mode. A flight mode that commands the autopilot to execute whatever flight plan is stored within its memory.

battery eliminator circuit (BEC). (Also known as voltage regulator.) An electronic circuit that accepts the input of the flight battery voltage and outputs a lower voltage to components that require it.

board camera. A compact, simplified camera that is usually mounted onto a small circuit board and that has no internal recording capability. These cameras are usually well-suited for FPV pilot camera applications.

breakout altitude. *See* safe altitude.

brushless motors. The motor that is the standard for RC aircraft propulsion. The term "brushless" refers to the fact that no electrical contact occurs between the stationary portion of the motor and the rotating portion, or bell. Therefore there is no "spark" between these two portions as might be observed in a brushed motor.

chord line. An imaginary line that bisects the airfoil, passing from the leading edge to the trailing edge. The chord line is used as a reference for determining lift and drag.

collective maneuver. The collective increase or decrease of thrust output by the propulsion system of a rotor-wing aircraft, usually used to produce altitude or speed changes. This phrase originally referred to traditional helicopter maneuvers but is also analogous to multicopter flight.

commanded state. The condition of the aircraft required to execute its mission or maintain stable flight in its current mode (e.g., heading to next waypoint, straight-and-level flight orientation, mission altitude setting, etc.).

control surface. Movable panels located on the trailing edges of the tail and outboard sections of the wings of a fixed-wing aircraft. These control surfaces include ailerons, elevators, and rudders and are used to vary the lift generated by the various aerodynamic surfaces of the aircraft to produce changes in roll, pitch, and yaw.

current state. The condition of the aircraft as measured by the flight controller sensors (e.g., pitch and roll attitude, GPS position, ground speed, etc.).

cycle power. The act of disconnecting and reconnecting power on a device. This is often the first and most reliable step in troubleshooting a piece of equipment, regardless of how expensive or complex it is.

cyclic maneuver. The vectoring of thrust output by the propulsion system of a rotor-wing aircraft, usually used to produce pitch and roll. This phrase originally referred to traditional helicopter maneuvers but is also analogous to multicopter flight.

drag. A force that opposes the movement of an aircraft through the air. Drag may be a byproduct of lift, a function of the cross-section of the aircraft, and/or friction between the air and the surface of the aircraft.

drone. An aircraft capable of autonomous flight but which cannot be monitored or controlled for most or all of its flight.

electronic speed controller (ESC). A component used to convert the direct current (DC) provided by the flight battery into the alternating current (AC) required to operate brushless motors.

endlap. The overlap of the surface footprint of sequential photo survey images. This overlap is determined by the interval between triggering of one image and the next and factors into post-processing quality.

failsafe system. In general, a means of protecting or attempting to save the aircraft in the event of an emergency or adverse event.

field kit. A collection of tools, materials, and equipment that allows operators to complete regular repairs and maintenance while in the field.

final approach glide slope. The angle of descent, relative to the ground, that a fixed-wing aircraft will usually attempt to maintain during final approach.

final landing descent rate. The final rate of descent, usually expressed in feet or meters per second, that a fixed-wing aircraft will attempt to maintain during final approach.

final landing transition altitude. The altitude above the ground at which a fixed-wing aircraft executing a landing action will transition from its initial to final glide slope and associated parameters.

first-person view (FPV). A technology that allows personnel on the ground to operate from the perspective of the aircraft in flight, with the first-person viewpoint displayed on a video monitor or video FPV goggles.

fixed mount. A payload mount that holds a camera or sensor at a constant orientation relative to the structure of the aircraft. These mounts may be "soft," incorporating vibration isolation to improve image quality. Fixed mounts may be used effectively in fixed-wing aircraft operating at high altitudes for photo surveys but are not recommended for rotor-wing aircraft.

fixed-wing aircraft. An aircraft that uses fixed, non-rotating wings to generate lift through forward airspeed. Commonly referred to as airplanes.

flare altitude. The altitude, usually only a few meters above the ground, at which a fixed-wing aircraft will execute a flare during landing.

flare throttle setting. The throttle setting that a fixed-wing aircraft will maintain after flare and immediately before touchdown. For most aircraft, this setting is idle.

flare. A subtle fixed-wing maneuver executed immediately before touchdown meant to ensure landing while also reducing the descent rate in order to lessen stress on the airframe. A flare is accomplished by increasing the aircraft's angle of attack to near the point of stall.

flight controller. A computer processor on board an aircraft that converts inputs, including user commands and sensor data, into outputs to the maneuvering controls for the purpose of maintaining stable flight.

FPV. *See* first-person view.

GCS. *See* ground control station.

geofence. The geographic area and altitude range in which the aircraft is safely allowed to operate, as specified by the user in the mission control software.

gimbal control unit (GCU). Functioning similar to a flight controller, a GCU has an internal accelerometer or IMU providing information about the aircraft's attitude, but it allows separate processing power to be devoted to stabilizing the gimbal at a high frequency. Often used to orient the camera.

gimbal. Also referred to as a stabilized mount, a gimbal uses its own IMU and actuators to stabilize a camera or sensor regardless of the orientation of the aircraft. In many cases, a gimbal may be pointed by the operator through dedicated RC channels.

Global Positioning System (GPS). A system used to determine the three-dimensional position (latitude, longitude, and altitude) of a receiver unit by referencing radio signals, transmitted by a constellation of geosynchronous satellites containing precise time codes.

go-around. The act of returning a fixed-wing aircraft to final approach following a wave-off in order to attempt another landing. An aircraft will usually attempt a go-around immediately after a wave-off unless the landing site is deemed unsafe or low battery voltage necessitates an immediate landing, both of which would require use of an alternate landing site.

ground control station (GCS). A collection of ground-based components required to operate unmanned systems safely and effectively. The GCS consists of an interface device, telemetry transmitter/receiver (transceiver), remote control transmitter (RC TX), payload interface, and power sources.

ground effect. A phenomenon that causes aircraft to generate lift more efficiently while extremely close to the ground. This may cause fixed-wing aircraft to prematurely climb before establishing a safe airspeed during takeoff or to "float" during landing, extending the total landing distance. Ground effect can also be observed in rotor-wing aircraft. The phenomenon is most prominent while less than a wing or rotor-blade length above the ground.

ground sample distance (GSD). A measurement of image resolution, specifically the distance between adjacent individual pixels in a photo of the Earth's surface. A smaller GSD equates to a higher level of detail in images.

imaging sensor payloads. A camera or other form of imaging sensor on board an unmanned aircraft. The three basic configurations of imaging sensor payloads are surveying, FPV reconnaissance, and FPV pilot camera.

IMU. See inertial measurement unit.

inertial measurement unit (IMU). An electronic device that can detect an aircraft's rate of acceleration and its rotation about the three axes (pitch, roll, and yaw). Also called accelerometer.

Land Now. A flight mode that will command a rotor-wing aircraft into a descent at a predetermined landing descent rate while maintaining GPS position. A fixed-wing aircraft in Land Now flight mode will usually begin a descending spiral at its current position until coming to rest on the ground.

landing descent rate. The rate of descent, commonly expressed in feet or meters per second, that an aircraft will usually attempt to maintain during landing.

landing direction. The heading that a fixed-wing aircraft will attempt to maintain during landing, leading down the length of the runway or landing zone.

landing roll limit. A limit imposed on fixed-wing roll, usually after flare, in order to touch down in a level orientation.

lift. A force, usually thought of as directed upward, resulting from a pressure differential created by a body with an airfoil cross-section moving through a mass of air.

LiPo batteries. Lithium polymer (LiPo) batteries are rechargeable batteries comprised of multiple cells containing lithium polymer. These batteries have become the power source of choice for small drone operators because of their high power density.

multicopter. An unmanned aircraft consisting of an arrangement of motors spinning attached propellers to generate vertical lift.

multiplexer (MUX). A switching device that can be installed on board an aircraft to allow the pilot to select between two sets of control inputs. In practice, such a device may be used to take RC control of the aircraft by taking the flight controller out of the loop.

on-screen display (OSD). The superimposition of aircraft telemetry data onto a live video feed.

PID. Proportional-integral-derivative algorithm. Almost all flight controllers utilize PID control loops to achieve control of the aircraft. Flight performance is dependent on the PID tuning and parameter setting of the autopilot.

power distribution board (PDB). A component that distributes the voltage of the flight battery to the many components on the aircraft.

power management units (PMUs). External modules specific to a flight controller system that can monitor voltage and current usage while also supplying regulated power to the flight controller.

prop. Abbreviation for propeller.

received signal strength indication (RSSI). A measurement of the strength or quality in a received radio signal.

receiver (RX). An airborne component installed on board an aircraft that captures signals broadcast by the corresponding transmitter.

remote control (RC) aircraft. Also called radio control aircraft. An aircraft, regardless of size, that is piloted solely by a person outside of that aircraft via some means of wireless communication.

remote control transmitter (RC TX). The handheld ground component of a remote control system that serves as the primary means of controlling the aircraft.

Return to Home (RTH). A flight mode in which the autopilot commands the aircraft to climb to a predetermined altitude and fly to its home position.

rotor wash. The artificial turbulence occurring immediately beneath a rotor-wing aircraft, generated by its own spinning propeller blades.

safe altitude. The altitude that a fixed-wing aircraft must reach after takeoff while subject to pitch, roll, and heading limits before it is free to maneuver to the first waypoint normally.

servo. An actuator device primarily used to physically move control surfaces on airplanes and to articulate swash plates on helicopters. Servos can also be adapted to move other aircraft components (e.g., landing gear, camera mounts, and bay doors).

sidelap. The overlap of the surface footprint of laterally adjacent photo survey images. This overlap is determined by the lateral distance between parallel photo survey legs and factors into post-processing quality.

Stabilize flight mode. A flight mode in which the aircraft will attempt to maintain straight-and-level flight (fixed-wing) or hover (rotor-wing).

stall. A condition characterized by the disruption of smooth airflow over an aerodynamic surface resulting from an excessive angle of attack. When a fixed-wing aircraft stalls, it is no longer able to generate enough lift to support its own weight and, depending on the aircraft's characteristics, this may result in a spin. The risk of stall is highest while airspeed is low, and stalls can be difficult to recover from while at low altitude, which can make takeoff and landing particularly critical.

swash plate. A complex mechanical device used to vary the pitch, and therefore angle of attack, of the main rotors of a traditional helicopter independently. The resulting changes in lift vector are used to produce attitude and thrust changes through cyclic and collective maneuvers, respectively.

take-off climb rate. The climb rate, usually expressed in feet or meters per second, that an aircraft will attempt to maintain during a takeoff action.

take-off pitch. The pitch angle, or angle range, that a fixed-wing aircraft will attempt to maintain during a takeoff action in order to achieve the most efficient climb, satisfy the climb rate and speed requirements, and also avoid stall.

take-off speed. The airspeed that a fixed-wing aircraft will attempt to maintain during a takeoff action in order to achieve the most efficient climb while also avoiding stall.

telemetry unit. A radio module that transmits and receives data, such as aircraft telemetry and operator commands, between the aircraft and the ground. One such transceiver is installed on the aircraft, and another is part of the ground control station.

thrust. The force generated by the propulsion system of an aircraft that moves it through the air. For a fixed-wing aircraft, thrust is directed longitudinally and moves the aircraft forward. For a rotor-wing aircraft, thrust is directed vertically and is directly related to lift.

touchdown pitch. The pitch that a fixed-wing aircraft will attempt to maintain after flare, resulting in a shallow descent immediately before touchdown.

touchdown point. The point on the surface of the Earth where the aircraft will attempt to touch down after completing a landing action. For a fixed-wing aircraft, this point will be located at the end of the glide slope and flare. For a rotor-wing aircraft, this point will be at the bottom of the vertical descent.

transmitter. *See* remote control transmitter.

unmanned aircraft (UA). An aerial vehicle that may be piloted remotely, similar to an RC aircraft, or fly autonomously, like a drone, due to its distinguishing feature: an onboard flight controller with a two-way data transmission system. This system facilitates communication between the aircraft and a ground station, allowing an external pilot to both monitor the aircraft's status (i.e., position, altitude, heading) and send commands to the aircraft in flight.

vertical takeoff and landing (VTOL). The capability of an aircraft (generally rotor-wing) to take off and land vertically as well as hover in place.

visual line-of-sight (VLOS). The range at which a pilot can maintain visual contact with the aircraft while also being able to successfully determine its heading and orientation. In practice, this is usually no more than 750 meters slant range.

visual observer (VO). A crewmember tasked with observing the aircraft at all times in order to assist the pilot-in-command of the operation.

VTOL. *See* vertical takeoff and landing.

wave-off. The act of climbing to abort a landing, usually by a fixed-wing aircraft. A wave-off may be necessitated by a safety hazard in the landing area or by a missed approach.

waypoint. A point in three-dimensional space, usually specified by latitude, longitude, and altitude, which the aircraft will attempt to pass through or within a specified distance of as part of an autonomous mission. A series of these waypoints may be edited by the user and uploaded to the aircraft to create an autonomous mission.

Index

motor set up, 73, 80
multicopters, 11, 12–15, 108
    airframe configurations, 12–14
    flight maneuvers, 14
    mission planning for, 132–137
    selecting components for, 62
    set up of, 68–81
multiplexer (MUX), 28, 83–86

O

on-screen display (OSD), 56, 57, 59–60
optical flow sensor, 43
overlap, 135–136

P

payload, 28, 62–65
payload operator, 58–60
payloads, 71, 139
    flight testing with, 109–120, 122
    imaging sensor, 53–62, 134
    mounting, 15
photo survey, 53, 134–136
    components for, 53
PID loops and tuning, 55, 90, 121–123
pitch, 5–6, 9–10, 14, 18, 19, 27, 29, 39, 42, 79, 84, 108, 123. *See also* touchdown pitch
pitch limits, 90, 117
pitch tuning, 109–110
pitot tube, 43, 70, 83, 141
power distribution board (PDB), 32–33, 49, 70
power management unit (PMU), 32, 42, 79, 83, 142
power on procedure, 140
preflight checks, 137–142
    power off, 137–139
    power on, 141–142
propellers, 12–15, 52–53, 138, 140
    balancing of, 52
    selecting, 62–65
proportional-integral-derivative (PID). *See* PID loops and tuning
pulse-width modulation (PWM), 5, 7–8, 44, 50, 58, 73, 85–86

R

radius mode, 93
range sensor, 43
RC Link Loss (failsafe), 87, 96, 97, 113, 120
RC transmitter, 27
receiver. *See* remote control receiver; video receiver
recovery, 28, 146–148
recreational use regulations, 100–101, 104
region of interest (ROI), 133
registration, small UAS, 104
regulations, 99–105
remote control (RC) aircraft, ix
remote control (RC) systems, 5–10
remote control receiver (RC RX), 5–8, 24–25, 39–40, 69, 74–76, 78–79, 82–86
remote control transmitter (RC TX), 2, 3, 5–10, 27, 40, 69, 74–79, 82–87, 140–143, 145
remote pilot certificate, 101–104
retractable landing gear, 15, 29, 144, 146
Return Home and Land, 96
Return Home, Loiter, and Land, 97
Return to Home (RTH) (flight mode), 36, 91, 112, 119
roll, 5, 6, 9–10, 14, 20, 27, 39, 42, 79, 84, 93, 123
roll limits, 90, 117
roll motor, 55
roll tuning, 109–110
rotor wash, 111, 133, 147
rotor-wing aircraft, 11, 92–93, 132–137. *See also* helicopters; multicopters
rudder, 6, 9, 10, 16, 19, 23, 27, 84

S

safe altitude, 126, 129, 132
safety, 105
    battery use and, 38
    during flight testing, 108, 114
safety gear, 150
servo configurations, 23–27, 45
servo connection, 5, 48, 49, 70–71, 72–73